Against My Will

SOPHIE CROCKETT

Against My Will

Groomed, trapped and abused.
This is my true story of survival.

HarperElement
An imprint of HarperCollins*Publishers*
1 London Bridge Street
London SE1 9GF

www.harpercollins.co.uk

First published by HarperElement 2020

1 3 5 7 9 10 8 6 4 2

A catalogue record of this book is
available from the British Library

ISBN 978-0-00-834773-4

Printed and bound in Great Britain by
CPI Group (UK) Ltd, Croydon

This   ™ paper

Fo   green

For Mammy – for always being there.

This book is dedicated to every woman who
has been failed by the system. We are all
survivors and must stand together.

'I may not be a lion but I am a lion's cub
and I have a lion's heart.'

Elizabeth I of England, Wales and Ireland

Author's Note

Recounting the events you are about to read has not been easy. As someone with Asperger syndrome and a sufferer of post-traumatic stress disorder, revisiting these episodes in my life has been a harrowing experience. Some events are like blocks in my head, others like a continuous flow. At times it has felt like someone else's life, or a dark movie. In order to protect the identities of innocent parties, where appropriate, some of the names have been changed.

Prologue

I woke at 7 a.m. to the same thought that hit me every morning. It wasn't just a bad dream. It was reality. I was in the same bedroom, in the same house, with the same monster sleeping beside me. My nightmare continued.

And, like every morning, the second sensation to hit me was how cold I was. I was naked, of course, because he hated me wearing clothes.

Then it registered how much my body ached. Not just the odd muscle twinge or stiffness, but bone-shattering, soul-searing agony. I had been sure he was going to kill me last night. He'd come close many times during sex: forcing my legs so wide I thought they'd snap out of their sockets; pushing my head so far into the pillow from behind that I nearly suffocated; tightening the grip around my neck until I was sure the breath that squeezed out would be my last.

But no. Here I still was. Surviving.

Sex makes it sound like it was consensual. Let's call it what it was. Rape. Repeatedly. Every day. That's what happens when you live with a psychotic sex maniac. He would be like a wild animal, sticking his fingers into my eyes, screaming into my face and trying to rip the hair out of my head. He was so violent I thought at times that my neck or back would break as he threw me around, all the time shouting his commands, 'Do this! Do that! You're not moving enough!' Then shoving me into the position he wanted. Me, compliant, lifeless almost – like the ragdoll he wanted me to be, my body covered in bruises and bite marks.

All the time I would think to myself, *Nothing lasts forever, nothing lasts forever, everything's got to come to an end.* That was the only thing that saw me through it, the mantra I kept repeating over and over and over.

It's got to stop at some point.

Everything comes to an end.

Nothing lasts forever. Nothing lasts forever.

On mornings like this, with another day in hell stretching out before me, it was hard to believe it wouldn't be like this forever. Every day seemed the same. Sex, humiliation, excruciating pain, the debasing of my very soul. Day after endless day.

The monster stirred beside me. He got up.

'Today's the day we die,' he said, calm but menacingly. He left the room and went downstairs.

My senses tingled. I forgot about the abject pain. He wanted us to die together. He told me that most days. Only he could decide when, where and how. He didn't want me to be with anyone else. It was part of his many contradictions. He wanted us to be together. Together, together, together. It was all I heard. He demonstrated this by making sure he was with me every moment of every day. And I mean every moment.

I wasn't allowed to go anywhere alone. He stuck to me like a leech, always touching me. If I needed to go to the bathroom, he insisted on coming, watching me or, worse, even urinating while I sat on the toilet. He wished we could be 'sewn together', and he carried me around like a baby and insisted on feeding me from his plate.

Now it was like being together in this life wasn't enough.

'Today's the day we die.' My mind buzzed with the possibilities of what he meant. Waiting around to find out seemed the least favourable option, but there was nowhere to run or hide. I thought about escaping out of the window. I was one floor up. I'd survive the fall and at least I would be out of the house. How far away would I be able to get before he came after me?

Before I could put any plan into action, he came up the stairs with the same Rambo-style hunting knife he had threatened me with before. His eyes flickered manically. He closed the bedroom door.

Oh my God, I thought, *this is it. I am going to die.*

'What are you doing?' I said, trying to reason with him, keeping my voice steady. 'Put it away now.'

He stood there naked, waving the knife in my face. I tensed, waiting for the lunge. Instead he grabbed hold of his genitals.

'I'm not big enough for you, am I?' he sneered.

Instinctively, I tried to move his hand away, but I grabbed the blade and sliced my hand open. He twisted me around and pinned me to the bed, his 16-stone frame crushing my body, which was barely half his size. I couldn't move from the neck down. He had the knife to my throat. Sweat was pumping off me. If I showed any fear, though, I was sure he would push the blade into me.

I tried to remain as calm as possible. I knew what he wanted more than this sudden blood lust. It was what he always wanted. Somehow I managed to talk soothingly, longingly – whatever it would take to instigate sex.

He released his grip, put the knife on the bed. While he was distracted I pushed the knife off the bed with my foot.

He grabbed me and put me in a headlock. We fell off the bed with such force it was sent flying across the floor on its wheels. He still had my head in his grip.

'I'll do anything, please,' I said. 'Just leave me alone.'

He got to his feet, still holding me around the neck, and dragged me downstairs. He was rambling about this fantasy he had of me being abused as a child. It wasn't true, but he would go on about it constantly.

'I wished I'd known you as a kid,' he panted. 'I would have totally fucked you.'

He was beyond sick. I kept trying to remain calm. I knew that showing any emotion would make this perilous situation even worse. I was shaking, though. My brain went dead. I felt numb, like I was not part of my body anymore.

Knock, knock.

What was that? There was somebody at the door. Thank God.

He answered it. It was Mum. Had she just happened to be passing? Had she sensed my distress? What a relief it was to see Mum's face, but I could see the worry in her eyes. She knew something serious was happening.

Don't say anything, Mum, I thought to myself. *Don't say anything.*

She reached in and tried to grab me.

'Come on, now,' she directed her words to him. 'Sophie is coming with me.'

'She's not going fucking anywhere,' he said, grabbing me by the back and pulling me in. He slammed the door shut and locked it.

'I'm going to get your father and sister!' I heard her shout.

He moved me towards the stairs, but I knew if I went up there I would never come down again.

'I need to go to the toilet,' I pleaded.

He came into the bathroom with me. I slowed everything down, trying to take as long as possible. He twitched impatiently.

My dad wasn't well. He had suffered a heart attack brought on, I told myself, by my refusal to leave this monster. Like my older sister, Leanne, and my younger brother, Jason, my parents had tried everything to prise me away from him, but they didn't understand coercive control. They didn't know how he had manipulated me, taken advantage of my extreme vulnerability. I might have been 17 when I met this 30-year-old, but I was effectively a child, which was the way he liked it.

Asperger syndrome had made me a prisoner of my childhood. When I finally ventured out into the real world I met a monster who wanted to keep me caged in his prison of darkness. He isolated me from the people I loved, convinced me he was good for me and then, when I realised the true extent of his evil, controlled me with violence and my fear that he would kill my family if I disobeyed his commands.

I had treated my family terribly, but now they were my only salvation. Luckily, they only lived a few streets away. It wasn't long before I heard them back at the door. I was afraid of what he might do, but the delay had momentarily calmed him down. To my relief he opened the door to them. The shock and fear in their eyes were clear to see – but so too was the determination to get me out of there. I was still naked.

'I need to go and get dressed,' I told them.

He followed me upstairs. In the bedroom he came so close I could smell his rank, stale breath.

'I could break your neck now and no one would know,' he whispered. His hands made a snapping motion.

This was not over. I knew that. Even if I managed to slip past him and out of the house, this was not the end. Not by any stretch of the imagination.

Chapter 1

A nursery school,
near Mountain Ash, 1996

I knew immediately something was wrong. It didn't look right and the second I took a sniff, *Oh my God*. It was disgusting. And they wanted me to drink this? No way.

I tried to explain to my teacher: this milk was not right. But she wasn't interested. It was like she didn't care. 'Drink it,' she said. And then louder still, 'Drink it!'

It tasted even worse than it smelled. To this day I can taste it. I only have to look at a milk bottle and it brings the horrid memories of that day flooding back. It is one of my earliest memories, but it is so vivid it's like it was yesterday. I was only three years old and in nursery.

Just being there terrified me. I hated being separated from my mum. I didn't like the other children, the noise they made and the fact that they came up to me asking if

I wanted to play. Every day the school provided milk for us to drink. Even on a good day it was warm and creamy and not very pleasant, but that day, even at such a young age, I could tell it was off. The other children gulped theirs down and went back to doing whatever it was they were doing. I sat there, trembling and crying, wishing it was over and I could be back in my mother's loving arms.

'I can't drink this,' I spluttered through sobs.

'Just drink it, Sophie!' the teacher said, getting more agitated. The louder she got, the more I cried. 'You're not leaving that seat until you drink it all.'

The only way to make this terrifying confrontation end was to drink the foul-smelling, rank-tasting liquid. Slowly, retching with every mouthful, I forced it down. Three hours later the teacher allowed me to move.

'There,' she said. 'That wasn't so bad, was it?'

She had no idea. I haven't been able to look at a glass of milk since, let alone drink one. I still bear the emotional scars.

By the time I was three it was already apparent that I was different. And to understand how I ended up in the clutches of such a monster when I was just a teenager, it is important to know the challenges of my childhood.

I was the second child of Stephen and Helen Crockett. They had met as teenagers in Mountain Ash, a former mining town in the Cynon Valley in south Wales. Helen was 17 when she got together with Stephen, who was two years older and worked as a labourer and was a reservist with the Territorial Army. She fell pregnant a year later and they married a short time after, and then Helen gave birth to Leanne, my older sister. Money was always hard to find and it was difficult to put food on the table, but theirs was a happy marriage and they've been together now for 36 years.

I came along in 1993 and immediately presented a host of new challenges for my parents. I cried a lot and was a very anxious baby. It couldn't have been easy for my mother, who fell pregnant again while I was still little. The birth of my brother Jason completed our family. For any parent, having two children under three would be testing enough, but our closeness in age only highlighted how peculiar I was.

My condition first showed itself through my anxiety over the smallest things. Leaving the house in general was a big deal. I would burst into tears. But doing something like going to get my haircut would turn into a massive experience. I would erupt in a hysterical outburst. It was like the terror someone might feel at having to jump out of an aeroplane. It was that frightening for me.

My mum and dad were always very supportive and tried their best to alleviate my anxiety, but they often found themselves on their own. The understanding of childhood behaviour and its underlying causes was very limited back then.

Our two grandparents – my grandfather on my dad's side and my grandmother on my mum's – did not get me at all. They couldn't begin to understand my problems. They just thought I was being silly.

'Look at Jason,' they used to say to me. 'He's younger than you and he's not making a fuss.'

That became a theme. At an early playgroup I was so upset that Jason had to hold my hand the entire time. The assistants were forever saying, 'Your brother's younger but he's looking after you. It should be the other way around.'

I would sit there crying, wanting to go home. I didn't want to be separated from my mum and I didn't want to interact with the other kids. I was aware of that from a very early age. I never played with other children. I just couldn't get it. I didn't like play, I didn't like being around strangers, I didn't like the smell of the building or the other kids being loud. It felt so enclosed: all the other kids screaming, the teaching assistants being near me. I just wanted to be left on my own. It was all too much.

The same went for the children in our street. My mother encouraged me to interact, but I just didn't like the idea of playing with them.

By the time I went to the nursery where my ordeal with the milk took place, it was the same. I didn't under-stand why I had to go to these places. Once there, I was able to calm down, and I grew a little more accepting of my surroundings as long as I was left alone. At playtime I used to sit and put different headbands on, looking in the mirror. The other children did try to involve me, but I preferred my own company. This probably doesn't sound very nice, but I found from a very early age that other children weren't the same as me. They didn't get me and couldn't understand why I simply didn't want to talk to them.

I would do anything not to go to nursery. I would deliberately fall down the stairs. My parents would rush to my aid and comfort me, and wonder how such a thing could happen. I always told them it was an accident. My appeals for attention didn't always have the desired effect, however. I used to stand on drawing pins and embed them into the heel of my foot. My mum would notice me hobbling around and ask what the matter was. When I showed her she scolded me for being so silly. Given that my older sister hadn't behaved in such a manner, it must have been confusing and distressing for them.

When I started primary school it was a nightmare. I didn't have any friends and nearly every aspect of it terrified me. It added vast amounts of pressure. I hated school so much because of the teachers' lack of understanding. School was the worst possible environment for someone with my anxieties. I hated the noise, the smells, the idea of so many people in such a small space. When a teacher showed me the toilets I immediately thought, I can't use that, something that's used by all these other people – no way. I developed a phobia of germs and using public toilets that I still suffer from to this day.

When we had to sit on the carpet we always had to sit next to someone – even that made me uncomfortable. I hated eating with everyone at tightly packed tables. Even when I wasn't hungry they made me eat it all. I didn't understand why I had to eat if I wasn't hungry. Why couldn't I just have something later? Why was everything so regimented, so forced and tense? I spent a long time looking out of the window, planning my escape so meticulously, although I never had the guts to actually try it.

Sometimes, during playtime, the teachers put a movie on, and if it was something I didn't want to watch, like the Mr Bean film, they made me sit and watch it anyway. I didn't understand why I couldn't do something else. I wondered what the point of it all was.

The way my brain worked was not compatible with the way the teachers taught. They hated it when I corrected them on something, and would shout at me. If I didn't understand something, they would keep repeating themselves but with raised voices.

It didn't help when a girl flooded the toilet and blamed me. Even though I protested my innocence, nobody believed me, so they made me sit in the corner for hours.

I was only six and I felt persecuted. My anxiety hit new heights. Every morning I erupted in violent rages, screaming, lashing out and holding on to doors. The thought of going to school made me so stressed that I was physically sick. My hysterics left me wheezing and out of breath. The doctor referred me to a chest consultant who diagnosed asthma and prescribed me multiple inhalers.

At school I wanted to be on my own. At home, at night time, it was the opposite. I didn't like being left on my own in the dark and I had trouble sleeping, often lying awake for most of the night. If I did eventually get to sleep, I'd suffer frighteningly real night terrors and wake crying and screaming. Mum took to sleeping with me to help comfort me. Every night before I went to sleep my mum and I clutched hands and she'd say, 'Hand to hand, together we stand.' When I couldn't sleep she'd sing to me until the early hours of the morning.

During the day I used to love carrying Mum's nightdress around with me because it had her 'Mammy smell' on it. I would breathe it in and it would comfort me. If I was having a really stressful night, my dad would take me downstairs and put old drama series like *Secret Army* or *I, Claudius* on the television until it was morning. This was especially hard for him, as he would then have to leave to go to work.

Despite their best efforts to soothe me, night time continued to be a particularly challenging time. My mother would routinely have to sleep with me in my bed until I was 16. I sometimes tried to copy her loving gesture. When Jason was still young, about four, he would climb into bed with me when it was time for his afternoon nap. I read to him and smoothed his hair until he went to sleep, just like my mother did for me.

My parents would take my brother and me to my grandfather's house in nearby Penrhiwceiber once a week for an hour or two, just so they could have some time on their own. My grandfather couldn't cope with me, though. If I didn't want to do anything, he made a big deal of it. And on the rare occasion when we spent the night there I would be walking up and down the landing because I couldn't sleep. He would yell at me, which just made me more anxious.

In the summer we would sometimes go to Porthcawl on the south-Wales coast and rent a caravan. It wouldn't be relaxing, though, as I had a massive sand phobia. My parents would worry about me the whole time. I would be anxious about going there. They tried to accommodate my brother because he liked doing all the fun stuff, like going to the arcades, while I would stay outside, terrified to go in because of the noise and lights.

Even family days out presented problems. Once, we visited a stately home, where guides showed you round and told you how things would have looked back in the day. The guides wanted to involve the children with costumes and activities, designed to bring the period to life. It was too much for me. I wanted to leave straight away.

If we visited somewhere, more often than not we would have to leave halfway through. My parents tried to calm me down at first, but when they could see I was getting increasingly anxious they realised it was better just to leave. Jason was always understanding of my situation, but Leanne found it harder to accept. Her attitude was similar to that of my grandparents: I was being indulged and my parents needed to be stricter with me. It led to a lot of tension between us.

Life wasn't always stressful, however. In the summer Mum and Dad would take Jason and me for chips from the local fish shop and go up one of the many mountains not far from us, perhaps Maerdy Mountain or Brecon, to eat them. On other occasions we would make a trip to Craig-y-nos country park to feed the ducks and swans. Jason would play football with my father in the field while Mum and I sat talking or just looking at the scenery. I enjoyed going out for walks in nature. We had a Dalmatian dog, Ben, and I liked taking him for a walk in the fresh air, listening to birdsong and watching the seasons change.

I used to love being taken to our local library in Mountain Ash. It was something my parents did with Jason and me every week. There was something so special about going in and choosing another new book to read. I would spend ages finding one. I looked forward to that day every week.

For my birthdays Mum would hold a little tea party with cake, but I didn't have parties like other children my age. There would just be a simple opening of the presents. I liked getting books, and I started collecting dolls. When I was very young I started collecting Cabbage Patch Kids dolls. I dressed them up in nightclothes and tucked them into a bed I made for them every night. As I got older I probably wasn't into the same toys and games as other children. I was into fairies and fantastical figures, especially those drawn by Brian and Wendy Froud, who worked on the puppets for *The Dark Crystal* movie and helped create the character of Yoda for *Star Wars*. I enjoyed using my imagination and playing on my own, but I also started to become aware of the world around me. At the age of five I regularly came home from school for lunch. One day Mum served me a chicken leg and chips. I stared at it, thinking.

'Mam,' I said, 'is this the leg of a chicken?'

'Yes.'

'An actual leg of an actual chicken?'

'Yes,' she said.

'I can't eat this,' I said. 'What do you call people who don't eat these things?'

'A vegetarian,' Mum said.

'Well, I'm going to be one of them.'

Since then I've never touched meat. Once I'd made that connection between animal and plate, I just thought, *Oh my God, no*.

I have massive respect for my parents because they didn't try to dissuade me or patronise me. They never lied to me, either, by serving something and telling me it wasn't meat. They just accepted it and told me the truth, even if it meant making something special for me at mealtimes. My grandparents, on the other hand, just thought they were indulging me. They thought they should be stricter. They would serve me food and claim it wasn't meat. I might have been young but I wasn't stupid. I knew it was.

I was a challenge, and not just for my family. Once I'd calmed down and accepted – to a degree, at least – that I had to be at school, I found learning came easily to me. I was the first in my class to write my name and the first to read a book. I wanted to push on and learn more, but the teachers just wanted to hold me back so the other children could catch up. Instead, I read whatever I could lay my hands on at home. A particular favourite was the *What Katy Did* series by Susan Coolidge, about a girl who is always getting up to mischief until a horrible accident leaves her bedbound. I loved the idea of a very big, close family unit and Katy and Clover, her sister, being best friends. It contrasted with my own experience, with our small extended family and an older sister I annoyed with my outbursts. Leanne and I might have struggled to form a really close bond anyway because of our age gap, but at times I felt she didn't seem to understand my anxiety. I think she thought I put it on to get attention. I also shut myself off with my reading. I enjoyed stories like *Heidi* and *Black Beauty* but quickly moved on to adult books, fiction and non-fiction.

Once I became interested in a subject it quickly turned into an obsession. Space intrigued me from a very young age. I just loved the idea of being so small in a huge solar system that never seemed to end. It gave me a feeling that the problems I was facing were not really a big deal, because look how small I was in the universe. I could gain a little perspective sometimes, which helped calm me down.

Another obsession was Queen Elizabeth I. I can't remember what sparked my interest, but I loved the fact that she was a strong woman who had opposition against her but always took on the challenge. She was the underdog who few people thought would rule, yet she became one of the most successful monarchs Britain has ever seen. I loved this particular quote: 'I may not be a lion but I am a lion's cub and I have a lion's heart.' She wasn't to be underestimated. I also loved the way she turned fashion into a power statement – she just screamed power – and the symbolism in Elizabethan paintings, which told people she was all-seeing and all-knowing.

It was during this obsession that my dad took me to Waterstones. When we asked about a book on Elizabeth, the assistant said, 'Do you want me to find you a children's book?'

'No,' I said. 'I want the one by David Starkey.' The historian had written a biography on the Tudor monarch to accompany a TV series.

I can still picture the look of surprise on her face. I was only seven. That year my dad also bought me my first copy of *A Christmas Carol* by Charles Dickens, and I would read it every Christmas.

As if my anxieties and eccentricities weren't enough for my family to contend with, I began to sense that there was more to the world around me than what other people saw. I started to have what can only be described as psychic experiences. Clearly, thanks to my anxiety, I was more sensitive to my environment than your average child. But it was more than that. I could sense that people were trying to reach me – that spirits were communicating with me. At first it scared me. I was hearing voices, feeling presences around me that other people weren't aware of. I told my parents, but they didn't understand and thought it was just my imagination. I knew this wasn't one of my obsessions. There was something to this. I was still a very young child when these experiences became more common and scary.

I sensed the spirit of an elderly lady who seemed to take delight in frightening me. One day I was sitting in my brother's pushchair in the passageway in our house when she kicked it full force and I was thrown into the front door. My mother came running.

'What have you done?'

'It wasn't me. It was the old lady,' I said.

The look on her face told me she didn't believe me. My parents weren't that open to the idea of spirituality at that time.

The elderly woman wasn't the only thing I experienced. I'd hear heavy boots walking up and down the stairs in the night, and the door would open on its own and shut again. Items in my bedroom would also rearrange themselves.

Trying to make sense of the spirit world was one thing. But for my parents, the real world was challenging enough and there were more pressing issues for them to contend with. My dad was starting to struggle. As well as working as a labourer on building sites, he had been doing shifts driving a taxi. There were times when I hardly ever saw him. But then he started to develop mental-health problems and had to give up work. Money had always been tight, despite his best efforts, and when he was no longer able to work we were under even more pressure. We became very poor. We couldn't afford the things other children take for granted, like ice creams on sunny days. Our coal was donated by charities. The council house we lived in was falling down, literally. The roof leaked and it was waterlogged. The council deemed it uninhabitable, so we went to the top of the housing register as a priority case to move. They found a house for us in Aberdare, another former mining town ten minutes' drive away. It meant moving schools.

We were assigned social workers to assess our general wellbeing. My parents discussed with them how hard it was getting me to go to school. Mum wanted me to stay at home, but they said I needed to be socialised and going to school would sort that.

There was only one school that would take both Jason and me, which was a bit of a trek from where we lived. There were schools closer to where we lived in Trecynon, but my parents were keen for us to be together. If I'd thought my time had been hard at my last school, it was nothing compared to this place. At first I thought it might not be too bad. My teacher was nice and showed me some compassion. But after I moved on to a new teacher, I was on my own. The rest of the teachers didn't even try to understand me. All it would have taken was a few little concessions on their part to alleviate some of my anxiety, but they weren't interested. In fact, it was the opposite.

I had developed a phobia of being in the water. Swimming wasn't compulsory but they liked to take us to the pool. I really didn't want to go. They made such a fuss about it. To people who love swimming, it might sound like I was just being difficult, but when you are that age and beset with crippling anxiety it is a big deal. They seemed to think I was just trying to get out of it. When they did eventually relent and say I didn't have to get in the water, they made me take my school books and sit by the side of the pool and do some work. I felt like such a pariah and thought I was going to be sick in the stifling heat and the clawing smell of chlorine.

I would have lunch in the canteen, where children were expected to eat everything on their plates. On one occasion I wasn't hungry so I left some food. One of the dinner ladies called me back.

'Sophie Crockett, you haven't finished!' she shouted. I tried to say I wasn't hungry but she wouldn't listen.

I burst into tears, ran out of the room and locked myself in the toilet, refusing to come out for the rest of the day. I must have spent three hours in there. I was too scared to come out until I could go home.

I hated school so much I would cry and beg my parents not to make me go back. At night I would lie awake sobbing at the thought of it the next day.

'Please don't make me!' I begged every morning. It led to terrible outbursts.

We now know that children with autism are prone to outbursts. Mine were nearly all related to school. I just hated it. I felt the school didn't care. They didn't have the patience. It was a horrible time.

I enjoyed schoolwork mostly, but mathematics scared me. I developed a big phobia around it, but the teachers didn't help. If I didn't understand something, instead of showing me a different way they'd show me the same way but louder. I thought, *You just said that and I didn't understand it.*

Every day at 11 a.m. our maths lesson began. As the time approached I started to stress. My mind would go blank and I'd panic when the paper was put in front of me. I used to hide in the toilets or, if I couldn't get out of the classroom, I would write down anything just to get it over with, and then my work would come back with a big cross on it.

There were two girls in the class who picked on me. At first they said if I helped them with English they would help me with maths. They used to copy my English work, but the teacher thought it was me copying them. The girls blamed me. It was always the same. No one would believe me. My maths didn't improve, and it got to the stage where I wouldn't come out of the toilets or I would get a headache and beg to go and sit in the library, where it was quiet.

The library became my sanctuary. It was there that I

confined myself when my class was away on a trip, the thought of which scared me. I read all kinds of books, including the *Ramayana*, the ancient Indian epic fable of heroism and tragedy, and several by Charles Dickens too. My favourite was *Little Dorrit*, his commentary on society's treatment of the poor. It might not be one of his most famous, but it's a very understated novel and, to me, a truly wonderful book.

I enjoyed reading poetry too, particularly the works of William Wordsworth. By the time I was eight I could recite all the lines to his most famous work, 'Daffodils', which many people know only by its opening line, 'I wandered lonely as a cloud'.

I spent so much time in the library that it became a running joke with the teachers. They'd walk past and make snide comments like, 'In the library again, Sophie?' They probably had no idea the effect their comments had on me, but it felt like they were mocking me and they wounded me deeply.

My whole school experience was exhausting. I never knew what might trigger my anxiety attacks. The uniform was polo shirts, cardigans and trousers, which I was happy with because I wasn't in the least bit fashion conscious and I liked the fact that everyone wore the same thing. In summer, however, the girls wore gingham dresses. I hated mine, as it wasn't the same as the other girls'. It was made of a looser fabric, and I was convinced it made me different when the last thing I needed was to give the other girls any excuse to single me out.

Despite all these issues, I was still one of the top students. The teachers might not have recognised it, but when the class sat a literacy test I scored the highest, with a reading age of 18. I was proud of my work and strived to do well, but my condition, or whatever it was that affected me so severely, was getting out of control. I was desperate to stay off school. Every day was a battle. Sometimes I would get to stay off or I would go every other day if I could be dragged in.

It got to the point where my mum and dad stopped forcing me to go anywhere. It seemed that the things other children enjoyed were denied to me because of my extreme anxiety. I was just locked in myself. I was nine years old and felt like an alien – that I didn't fit in with this world around me. And on top of that was my belief that I could see spirits around me and hear what they were saying. People seemed to be contacting me, telling me they had passed on. They appeared before me. It was scary. Why were they communicating with me? It was a deeply disturbing and difficult time.

Against this backdrop of worsening behaviour, my parents, who had been trying to keep my issues secret, hoping it was a stage I'd eventually grow out of, decided to ask for help. They went to the doctor I had seen about my asthma. He referred me to a mental-health team, and for a while I was seen by a number of psychiatrists all over the region. One suggested I take Ritalin, the drug used to treat children with attention deficit hyperactivity disorder, while another suggested I start the contraceptive pill to stop me from going through puberty. My parents flatly refused.

It felt like no one had an explanation. That was until we were referred to Dr Latif, an expert in autistic spectrum disorders at the University Hospital of Wales in Cardiff. I felt incredibly anxious and worried before I saw him, as I did with anyone I didn't know. My legs were actually knocking together and my hands were shaking.

I had a habit of walking on my toes, as I didn't like the feel of my heels on the floor, and as soon as I walked in he pinpointed it straight away: 'You have Asperger syndrome.'

He asked me a couple of questions, but I couldn't answer him, as I had terrible difficulty in communicating with strangers at the time and I couldn't make eye contact. This only seemed to confirm his diagnosis.

Asperger syndrome, or Asperger's, he explained, is a form of autism. People who have it are often above average intelligence but can display learning difficulties. As with other forms of autism it is a spectrum condition, so while people with it might share certain challenges, it will affect them in differing ways.

'With Asperger's,' he said, 'you will see, hear and feel the world differently to other people.'

That immediately struck a chord. Here, finally, was someone who understood what I was going through. I could see the relief on my mum's face. Throughout my childhood she had shown nothing but unconditional love, but there were many times when she'd questioned what exactly was the matter with me. We had all wondered, many times. Now there was an explanation.

Dr Latif explained that although Asperger syndrome was something I would have for life, and was not a condition that could be cured, it could be managed. It was a fundamental part of my identity that needed to be accepted and understood.

He gave my mum advice on how to manage the condition and advised her to buy books on Asperger's. He said he would write to the school explaining the diagnosis and advising ways in which they could help alleviate my anxiety.

At last there was a name for what I had. The impact that had on me was massive. Maybe I wasn't such an alien after all. Surely this would make a difference, I thought. My teachers would understand, the other children might begin to accept me more. It could be a new beginning for me. It was a massive relief for us all, because now my parents could get help. They had been in the dark until then, but now they thought, *Okay, it's a condition we can read about and get our heads around.* The more they read about the condition, the more they felt reassured, as I had all the key traits of Asperger's.

Any optimism we had was sadly short-lived. My mum and dad got in touch with an autism support group. I went along hoping it might be a chance to meet people in a similar position, but it wasn't like that. Autism covers a broad spectrum and I didn't feel the people there were like me at all. I still found it hard to relate to them. It was as if the imaginary barrier that stopped me from interacting with other people was still in place.

Autism understanding in society was still in its infancy. Progress was being made but the pace was slow for those of us going through it. A form of help was there, but if you couldn't cope with that, there was no alternative. As for my school, we persevered, hoping they would implement some kind of strategy to make my time there bearable. But it was no use. I felt very depressed.

However, one of the benefits of getting an Asperger's diagnosis was that my parents could look at other options – like home schooling. Eight months after our first meeting with Dr Latif, a plan was in place. I would never have to go back to school again. Instead I'd be tutored at home, potentially offering an end to the anxiety that had crippled my development so far.

I was thrilled. I was convinced that this would signal a new start, a chance to live a better life.

I couldn't have been more wrong.

Chapter 2

This was the life. No school, no horrible teachers or girls picking on me. A chance to push on at my own pace, no longer shackled by the limitations of the curriculum or held back by the slowest in the class. And, most importantly, it was the solution to my ever-increasing anxiety.

That was the dream, anyway. The reality was very different.

Although it was a blessed relief not to have to go into school, provision for home schooling was very limited. The local authority just did not know how to handle it. They could only provide a tutor for one hour every day. As I was technically still of primary-school age, it meant they sent teachers for my age, not my capacity.

I was ten but already reading challenging adult books and developing what would become a lifelong passion for Russian literature, especially works by Fyodor

Dostoevsky and Anton Chekhov. I read Shakespeare and, although on the whole I thought he was overrated, I enjoyed *Macbeth*. This was purely down to the character of Lady Macbeth, who I saw as a very strong, determined woman who knew exactly what she wanted and how to use her husband to get it.

I continued to develop interests in a variety of topics. My fascination with strong women extended to Emmeline Pankhurst, the political activist whose inspiring work helped women win the right to vote. The women's rights movement fascinated me and sparked a passion inside me for activism. Being outside of the school environment meant I grew a little braver about venturing outside of my comfort zone. I got involved with Animal Aid, leafleting around the town for issues like animal testing and writing for its children's paper on why I decided to become a vegetarian. My dad accompanied me as I went from door to door. I think he respected me for wanting to do something to try to change people's attitudes.

All of my knowledge came from reading and forming my own opinions. I didn't watch television. Most children are happy to plonk themselves in front of the box, but for as long as I can remember I've viewed television as a form of brainwashing. I had the same disdain for games consoles. My sister and brother loved playing computer games, but I thought they were a waste of time.

I was content with my doll collection. These were antique twentieth-century dolls, not for playing with but to display. I wasn't interested in contemporary television programmes. I preferred learning about history and was intrigued by the elegance and style of other periods, not in Britain but abroad – like the lavish costumes worn by Marie Antoinette, the last French queen before the revolution, or the Japanese geishas and how their clothing and make-up changed depending on their seniority and experience. I even dabbled in making my own jewellery.

For a while I was the happiest I'd ever been. Left to my own devices, I could be content and amuse myself. Within the family there was greater understanding of how I saw the world. But that didn't mean there wasn't the odd blow-up. Attempts to include me in family activities still often ended in tears. I remember going with my dad, brother and sister to the cinema to see the animated movies *Ice Age* and *Monsters, Inc.* Most people would just think of these films as harmless family fun, and I did try to enjoy them, but the reality was that I couldn't stick the cinema; it was too sensory, too dark and loud, too in-your-face. I accept that it wasn't fair on my brother and sister, but I just wanted to leave. So that was it. We all had to. It caused a bit of tension, understandably, but we were all still trying to come to terms with my Asperger's and working out ways to manage the extreme reactions I had.

One place I enjoyed going to, where I didn't experience anything like the same blow-outs, was the ballet. The Coliseum Theatre, which hosted regular performances, was close to where we lived. Going to watch the dancers move with such grace and elegance captivated me. I loved classical music as well. It reflected and influenced my moods. And I liked the reserved atmosphere of the theatre. I felt like I was entering a different world, one that did not impose itself on me.

My parents were delighted that I'd found something I could enjoy without feeling anxious. They had almost given up on trying to get me involved in some sort of activity or club. I was not sporty and anything that involved interacting with other children was not an option. When they asked if I wanted to take up ballet-dancing lessons I felt excited, but the thought of being in a class with other girls who might judge and look down their noses at me filled me with fear. My parents investigated, however, and found a dance teacher who was willing to offer private lessons. It would just be the teacher and me, no other children to stress or distract me. I was nervous at first. The thought of anything new brought out the old anxieties, but I loved watching ballet so much that the prospect of actually learning how to dance like that was a magical dream.

The teacher was firm but encouraging, and once I got over my initial nerves I started to really enjoy the lessons.

I pleasantly surprised everyone by how easily I picked it up. As with my other obsessions, I threw myself into the practice 100 per cent. It was blissful respite from my everyday existence.

I continued to have my psychic experiences. I could feel, see and hear spirits. This continued to concern my parents, who had hoped it was a passing phase and thought it was just my imagination running away with me. They didn't understand it, but I was becoming more intuitive and they couldn't really deny it anymore. To people who don't believe, it might sound strange, but I could see angels. They appeared before me, and just as people might imagine; I could see their wings. The one I saw most often was my mother's guardian angel, called Jasmine. I saw her wearing a pink dress. She had long, brown curly hair with flowers in it and her wings had pink tints to them. She had a calming presence about her.

Some of the spirits were from relatives of mine who had passed on, but often they had no connection to our family. Sometimes the spirits had messages from the other side. I would amaze people by saying something only they would know. For example, my father's mother always called him 'Chick' as a child, and nobody but him knew this. When I said, 'Granny says, "Hello, Chick,"' he was flabbergasted.

As with my autism, the longer it went on, the more my parents thought they'd better seek an expert opinion.

Paul Hanrahan was a well-known medium from a television programme called *Ghost Detectives* and also a friend of a friend of my grandmother. They got in touch and he came to meet me. I was quite anxious because this was someone new. I didn't speak to him but he looked at me intently.

'You have a very, very bright light,' he said. 'You're incredibly gifted psychically.'

He told my parents he knew of spirits at this location and that he too had seen them just as I had described them.

'Sophie is a very special person,' he told my parents. 'She's clearly an indigo child. To be as gifted psychically is rare.' People can see things all the time, yet they always doubt their senses, but he believed I was clairvoyant, someone with supernatural ability; clairsentient, as I could feel psychic energies; clairaudient, capable of hearing messages; and claircognisant, an ability to sense the future. He said I possessed a very rare gift, but he wasn't in the least surprised. Many children can display spiritual powers.

Indigo children, he explained, are supremely empathetic, curious and strong-willed – traits I had already demonstrated – and often considered strange by other adults and their peers. The concept of indigo children had been coined in the 1970s by a psychic, after the colour of their aura, but it had gained credibility since the 1990s. Once my parents better understood what I was capable of, they began to embrace it.

I got more and more into spirituality. I learned how to read tarot cards. I began using a dowsing crystal to tap into my sixth sense and answer questions that were puzzling me. I could see people's auras and learned how to interpret the different colours to tune into their emotional energy. And because I felt the presence of spirits, I became something of a psychic medium, doing readings for people using messages I was hearing. I gave readings to my mum, dad, aunt, grandmother and even a great-uncle who I never saw. After I had a dream about a lady who said her name was Glenis, my mother told my grandmother, who immediately recognised the significance. Glenis was my great-uncle's wife. I had never heard of her or seen any photographs of her, but I described her exactly as she was. Since that day my great-uncle believed in spirits.

We found out there was a church in Ferndale, about a 15-minute drive away over the valley in Rhondda, which held spiritualist meetings. We paid it a visit and the people there were really nice and welcoming. We started to go quite regularly, and it became a little outing for my brother and me. I felt quite at home there and enjoyed the singing, the prayers and the psychic readings.

Paul Hanrahan even wanted me to join his psychic circle – a group of like-minded experts who gave spiritual readings. I was still only ten years old, though, and due to my condition this wasn't an option.

I was in a contented place. Two years on from my Asperger's diagnosis and a year after quitting school, I was feeling a little less anxious and quite optimistic about life in general. Sadly, it would not last.

It was approaching Christmas when my dad and I went out to go shopping for presents for my mum. From out of nowhere a car appeared in front of us at a junction. There was nothing my dad could do. We crashed into it, the impact throwing me forward. My head exploded in pain. I was so shocked at first that I didn't know what had happened. When I came to my senses I realised my face had smacked off the airbag that had inflated on impact. My dad was slumped forward on his.

Oh, good lord, I thought. *Please, no.*

I couldn't breathe between sobs. I thought he was dead. Within seconds, though, he started to come round. My nose was in agony. The medics who were quickly on the scene confirmed it was broken. And when they told me Dad was going to be okay I began to calm down, but I was badly shaken. When we'd had time to digest what had happened we realised there was nothing my dad could have done. The other driver had just pulled out in front of us. She appeared unhurt.

Our physical scars soon healed, but the incident would have psychological repercussions for years to come. The woman initially denied responsibility for the accident, and we were lucky that a group of builders working on a house nearby saw what had happened and told the police they'd seen her pull out without looking.

After thinking I could control my anxiety, that incident sent me backwards. Whenever my dad left the house I was terrified he would be in another accident. My GP said I was suffering from post-traumatic stress disorder. After the legal wrangling that followed I was awarded a significant sum in compensation, money that would be held in a trust for me until I turned 18. It was one positive to take from the highly distressing incident. And then another episode unsettled me even further.

One of my home-school tutors was an older woman called Mary who took a shine to me. She was in her sixties, and dressed quite shabbily, though she lived in a large house in Pontypridd, about 12 miles away. While some other teachers just turned up, took me through some exercises and left, Mary was intrigued by me. She saw potential in me that no other teacher had recognised before, and was amazed by my reading capacity and intelligence for my age. She was more willing to move away from the curriculum and have more meaningful conversations about a broad range of topics. I enjoyed her visits and thought, finally, here was someone who understood me.

But then it took a turn.

Mary invited me to her house for a change of scene and wanted to take me to the theatre. My mum and dad were concerned she was overstepping the mark, but they were afraid to say the wrong thing so went along with it. Mary was getting me out of the house, after all. It was surely a positive thing, right?

Mary was very snobby. She would make comments about shelf-stackers in supermarkets as though they were beneath her and talked about 'stupid' people. She was quite a eugenicist, who would have happily seen certain types of people discouraged from reproducing. She started to become fixated with me, weirdly obsessed. When we were alone she said, 'You know, Sophie, you are better than your parents. You could achieve so much more if you weren't with them.'

I had been flattered when she'd made comments about how special I was, but this was too much. It was like she was trying to turn me against my family.

Once, when she was in our house, she spied my mum and dad's magazines on the table. She picked them up and said, 'Who reads books like this, Sophie?'

'My parents, but I occasionally glance through them as well,' I said, feeling defensive.

'Yes,' she said, 'but you wouldn't buy them now, would you?'

She made comments about the many photographs of pets we had in frames on the wall, saying it was weird and they should be confined to photo albums. And she used to discourage me from engaging with my mental-health nurse, who she thought was a 'stupid, blonde bimbo'.

She thought I was a very gifted child who needed specialist care. Without my family's permission she got in touch with Christ College boarding school in Brecon to enquire about me going there. I knew she was a bad influence and she made me feel uncomfortable, but I grew attached to her because she was the first person to help me get my confidence back in my academic abilities.

Then she wanted me to go to London with her and stay with her son. It all started to get creepy.

'I wish you were my granddaughter,' she told me. 'We would be able to spend a lot more time together and I could teach you so much about the world.'

It was like she saw me as a way to fill a void in her life. One day the snow was so bad she couldn't get her car out, so she wouldn't be able to keep her appointment to see me. But rather than accept it, she walked the ten miles in the driving snow to my house just to see me for a couple of minutes.

That was the final straw as far as my parents were concerned. They could see that an extremely unhealthy relationship was developing. They spoke to one of the psychiatrists who'd seen me about my anxiety attacks.

He immediately agreed with them that it was weird. He reported what was going on to the local authority and Mary stopped coming to the house after that. We were glad to bring an end to what was a strange episode, but it was unsettling.

Mary had a strange energy around her, and it was disturbing to think that someone could come to my home and fixate on me. Already it was clear that I had attracted some obsessive characters. But it was to get a lot worse.

Chapter 3

Blending steely determination with more than a little natural grace, I moved through the ballet moves, concentrating hard to maintain perfect posture throughout. Glissade through assemblé to relevé, I loved the combination of discipline and elegance, and the pursuit of producing something beautiful.

'Excellent, Sophie,' my dance teacher said. 'You move beautifully. Well done.'

Ballet was such a revelation for me. I felt that I belonged there. The long trips to the school didn't faze me, and for a couple of years I loved dancing. I quickly reached quite a high standard, practising hard to pass my exams and move through the grades. It seemed like no time before I was dancing en pointe, just like the ballerinas I'd so admired at the Coliseum. I was enjoying it so much that I was even looking ahead and considering going to the prestigious Northern Ballet School in

Manchester to continue my development, even though it was precisely the type of leap into the unknown that would usually have had me panicking. That's how seriously I was taking it.

That was until one day, when my teacher sat me down on the floor and said, 'You could be such a good dancer, Sophie,' she paused, her eyes scanning my already slender frame, 'if you lost some weight.'

She said it so very casually, like it was just another step I had to learn. For any girl to be told that – even one without autistic traits – is dangerous. Some people might be able to brush off a comment like that and not take it seriously. Someone like me, however, prone to obsessive behaviour and with an addictive personality, immediately took it to heart.

I went home and looked at myself in the mirror. Anyone else standing beside me would have seen a thin little girl. But as I examined myself I thought, *Maybe she has a point*. I pulled at my stomach and examined my arms and legs. Had I got fatter? I wanted to please my teacher. If I wanted to become a proficient dancer then I had to take on board what she said.

Okay, I thought, *I have to lose weight.*

My confidence in my body was already shaky. I had a keen interest in fashion and at one stage dreamed of being a model, but there were parts of my body I had issues with, and wearing a leotard and tights in a room full of mirrors, you notice these things more. I admired very skinny models and ballet dancers and had in my head the quote by George Balanchine, co-founder of the New York City Ballet and one of the world's most influential choreographers: 'You can only dance if you can see the bones.'

My teacher was always quite intense. She was so strict she could have been straight out of a Russian ballet company. I liked her discipline, though, and I responded to the challenges she set for me. She used to be a dancer and still choreographed for a ballet company. She knew what it took to reach that standard. I wanted to be a dancer, just like her, which was why I took her very seriously when she made those comments and others about the way I looked.

I didn't tell anyone about our conversation or how I was thinking, but in the days and weeks that followed I started to look at the food put in front of me. Suddenly it didn't look like a wholesome, nutritious meal, lovingly prepared by my mum anymore. Instead, I imagined every morsel adding rolls of lumpy fat to my body. It was completely irrational, I know, but it seemed a perfectly sensible attitude at the time. I began calorie-counting everything, cutting out any treats and limiting myself to around 500 calories per day.

I thought I was doing well, but not long after, when I arrived for my lesson, my teacher's eyes scanned my body again. I immediately felt self-conscious. Had I overindulged? I thought I was being good. How did she know? Was it that obvious? I went home even more determined to show her that I could lose weight – and fast.

At night I exercised in my bedroom, doing hundreds of sit-ups and press-ups. But when I checked myself again in the mirror it wasn't enough. I just looked the same. I sat down on the floor feeling wretched. I needed to do more. I went into the bathroom, took my toothbrush and shoved it as far as it would go down my throat. I gagged at first; I wasn't sure if I could go through with it. I pushed it further back. That did the trick. I slumped over the toilet as my stomach emptied into the pan. That was much better! I was now far more pro-active in my quest for skinniness.

At first no one noticed. You can get away with saying you're not hungry or that you've ruined your appetite by eating too many snacks during the day. Quickly, though, like the other things in my life I'd become fixated on, it became an obsession.

I started picking at my food, cutting it into small pieces, making it look like I was tucking in as normal, but when no one was looking I discreetly tipped it into the bin. I'd take meals up to my bedroom when I could. Food became the enemy. I hated the idea of eating anything. I used to look at my meals, things I'd previously loved eating, and think, *No, I don't want to eat that, think what it will do to me – no way.*

As I starved myself of nutrients and energy, I became lethargic and ill. That helped because the first thing to go when you feel off colour is your appetite. The weight dropped off me. I was always slender but soon I was really skinny. Still it wasn't enough. Whenever I looked in the mirror, all I'd see was a fat girl.

I wrote notes to myself about how big I was and took a marker pen and scrawled on my stomach the word 'Fat'. I wrote the same on my arms and legs, on any part of my body I didn't like. If I felt hungry I looked at the words and I wouldn't eat.

At dance class I hoped my teacher would notice the effort I was making. She did and praised me for it. One weekend, though, I lost control and ate a treat. At my next lesson she somehow knew.

I started logging on to pro-anorexia websites, where I found a raft of clever ideas – despicable, of course, for a young girl to view, but when you have an eating disorder your personality changes completely and these disturbing websites spoke to the new me. I imagined food as vomit or being maggot-infested. I brushed my teeth right before having to eat in an effort to put me off my meals. If I felt really hungry, I punched myself in the stomach – punishment for it making me feel that way.

During one mealtime my parents got suspicious and encouraged me to eat up. I kept saying, 'I am not hungry,' over and over. They had a go at me, telling me I was wasting away. To keep them off my back I ate everything on my plate. As soon as I was done I rushed to the bathroom and reached for my toothbrush. I started to gag and then brought my entire dinner back up. That felt good. Like I was winning.

Even though I was getting weaker and weaker, I kept pushing myself, both to do well at ballet and to get even thinner. My parents reached out to the mental-health team, which had previously supplied the psychiatrists to assess my anxiety attacks. A crisis team came to visit me at our house.

A mental-health nurse tried to offer practical solutions. 'Why don't you join a gym?' she said. 'That would help you gain confidence and reinforce positive connections with food, because it provides the energy you need to be healthy.'

It looked like she was helping, but my parents weren't present for what else she said.

'You know, Sophie,' she said, when we were alone, 'there are parts of my body I don't like. I hate my thighs, for instance.'

She was probably just trying to help by showing that most people have insecurities over their bodies, but I looked at her and saw someone really thin already. Her words had the opposite effect. They reinforced my own attitudes.

A psychiatrist I saw told my mum and dad to follow me upstairs after a meal and sit outside the door in case I made myself sick. This didn't help either, as it made my toilet phobia worse. And being pushed to eat just made me detest mealtimes even more, which led to huge arguments with my parents, as they were so concerned about me and didn't know what to feed me or what to do.

The psychiatrist also advised them to remove all the mirrors from the house because every time I looked in one I saw a huge, obese creature looking back. It didn't make much difference; even though I was getting so thin I felt constantly ill, I still thought I was fat. In my mind the weight loss wasn't happening fast enough. Without mirrors to examine myself in, I obsessively checked myself against my clothes, and was elated when I got a size-four top and it was a little too big for me. I felt so happy then – but still it wasn't enough. I was addicted to losing weight.

My actions seem crazy and irrational to me now, but back then I was locked into a course of action and nothing would persuade me otherwise. I ordered diet pills over the Internet without my parents knowing. At night I lay in bed stroking my hip and rib bones, feeling pleasure that I was achieving something.

My health rapidly deteriorated further. I felt dizzy and struggled to concentrate on anything for any length of time. My schoolwork suffered. As I entered my teenage years I didn't much rate my tutors anyway. After the episode with Mary, the local authority sent me primary-school teachers who again taught me according to my age rather than ability, and I felt stifled and uninspired. It didn't help that I continued to starve myself and immediately ran to the bathroom to throw up if I did eat a meal. If I had to go outside, I carried a toothbrush in my bag in case I needed to stick it down my throat to bring up anything I'd eaten.

My parents were at their wits' end – first the anxiety, then the overly attentive tutor and now this. An eating disorder, the kind of thing they'd only read about or watched on television. Yet here it was, happening to their daughter, and they felt powerless to stop it and even less able to understand it.

They took me to the doctor. He saw I was in the grip of anorexia nervosa and bulimia, but also said I was clinically depressed – bipolar, in fact – capable of experiencing highs but also devastating lows. He suggested putting me on medication. No way! Ever since I was a young child I'd had a phobia about taking drugs. There was no way I was putting pills down my throat.

He was right, though – I was depressed. I was sinking deeper and deeper into a black hole of my own making, because my addictive personality had latched on to my teacher's negative attitude to food. Still, I didn't let on to my parents or the health professionals about the root cause of my behaviour, and so we kept going to ballet.

Yet rather than praise me for my dedication, my dance teacher turned on me. One day I couldn't get on my pointes enough – probably due to a lack of energy because I was so skinny. She grabbed me by the hips and shoulders and shook me. I came home feeling broken, my body covered in bruises.

Ballet was no longer fun. It had been the only source of joy in my life, but it had turned sour. I sank lower. I hated ballet, I hated my teacher, but worst of all I hated myself. I hated the fact that I was the way I was. I hated being condemned to forever living as a prisoner to my condition. I wasn't in control; I was at the mercy of the Asperger's that ruled my mind. I hated my life. I felt cursed. If I was in tune with the spirit world, it wasn't able to help me. Medication wasn't the answer. I needed to find something else to relieve the pain in my head, to ease the blockage of self-loathing.

I felt an overwhelming need for release. Instinctively, I went to the bathroom and saw one of my dad's Bic razors. I pushed it against my leg – to my eyes the flesh-iest part of my thigh, even though it was stick thin. I pushed the blade deeper into my leg, watched as it broke the skin. It felt good. It was exactly what I needed.

As the blood oozed from the perfect cut it was like a valve had been opened, and all the tension was seeping out of me. It was amazing. I had never heard of self-harming. I wasn't even aware it was a concept. I just knew I'd found something that eased my pain.

But, like my quest to be as thin as possible, my desire to cut myself became an obsession. I gouged my skin at every opportunity. Every time I cut myself I told myself I deserved it. It wasn't like punishment, though. This was so, so sweet. I could breathe again.

I had a compulsion. Every time I got stressed I'd reach for the razor blade. It got to the point where I carried a razor blade in my handbag just in case. I always made the cuts on my leg because I could cover them up. I certainly wasn't doing this for attention. That was the last thing I wanted. I never showed anybody my scars. I was ashamed of them. I didn't want anyone to know what I was doing.

Once I got into it, I did quite a lot of damage. I got carried away, slicing and searching for patches of virgin skin. I was a mess, physically and mentally.

I turned to poetry, penning my own verse to try to put my pain into words. One poem from that time was called 'Maze of the Mind'.

Distorted image that was once so true.
Failure to recognise oneself.
Loathing of this shell I carry.
Losing my inner self.
Which image is honest?
Which image is truth?
Am I not as real as you?

My mind is a maze of twists and turns.
That no longer has substance.
A nothingness has sucked life dry.
A blackness has engulfed me.

Mental suffocation but physically well.
Screaming in frustration yet sitting calm and
    still.
'How are you?' they say.
'I'm well,' I reply.
But I feel already dead.

Being in such a distraught state presented the perfect
opportunity for a predator to pounce. My psychic senses
might have been clouded to any potential danger, but
someone else claiming to have spiritual powers spied an
opportunity to prey on an impressionable victim.

Chapter 4

It looked harmless enough. Fun, even. And I hadn't exactly enjoyed many fun times before we paid a trip to Brecon. I was with my parents and sister, and my primary reason for going there was to visit a bookshop. On the opposite side of the street was a spiritual crystal shop hosting a fair for all kinds of psychic practices. My kind of place, surely?

Once we went inside I saw that a psychic artist, who I will call Phil, was offering readings through art.

'I'd like to get this,' I said.

My parents shrugged and said it was fine, if that was what I wanted. Phil seemed perfectly nice and showed me upstairs to a small room where he did his artwork, while my family waited downstairs. He talked quietly and asked me some questions to get a sense of who I was so he could tune in and contact my spirit guide. He asked for some personal information, my name and phone number. I gave these to him without thinking much of it. Phil then explained that he would tune in to my spirit and channel it through his artwork.

I sat there, quite intrigued. He was sketching the figure of a man, but with large wings. As he was drawing he edged closer and closer towards me. I felt uncomfortable so I got up. He stood up too and I backed against the wall. He moved right in front of me, his large frame blocking the stairs. I started to feel scared. He was so close I could feel his breath on my face. He put his hand against the wall next to my head.

'You're a very special girl, Sophie,' he said, pinning me against the wall.

I didn't know what was going on. But I knew this wasn't right. Before he could do or say anything else, I slipped under his arm and ran down the stairs. My parents were still there, waiting for me.

'What's wrong?' my dad said, seeing the look on my face.

'I don't know,' I said, truthfully. I really didn't know what had just happened.

I looked back up the stairs and Phil was there holding the drawing. 'Sophie, you forgot your picture,' he said.

He came down casually behind me, smiling as if nothing had happened. He chatted to my dad a little bit about mundane things and said everything went well. All the time I just wanted to get away.

On the journey home my parents could sense something was wrong. They kept asking me what, but I just replied, 'I don't know.'

Back at the house I looked at his half-drawn picture to see what meaning I could glean from it. Not much. A short while later my phone buzzed with a message. It was Phil. He asked how I was and said he was sorry I ran off. Why was he contacting me? He knew I was only 14, but I looked much younger. I was confused. My brain couldn't work out whether it was normal for a middle-aged man to contact a young teenage girl. Shut away in my house, with none of the interactions with boys that other girls my age might get at school and parties, I was completely naïve.

It didn't feel right, but I didn't know what to do. I texted him back: 'I'm fine.'

The texts kept coming. He said he liked me, that he was sorry he hadn't been able to finish his sketch. He said he was only trying to help me. He had seen something special in me and wanted to help me understand more about what it meant.

I suppose I was flattered that this older man was paying attention to me. But it made me uncomfortable. This couldn't be how normal people behaved, could it? What was normal anyway?

I was still in the grip of my eating disorders and depression, so to become withdrawn and quiet wasn't new, but still my parents sensed something else was going on. They asked me repeatedly what was up, but I said nothing. I was too scared to tell them about what had happened upstairs at the spiritual fair or the texts. Maybe they would blame me. Maybe I was doing something wrong.

The texts became more frequent and the tone changed. Phil was clearly fascinated by me.

'Can you send me some photos of you,' he said in one text.

I didn't want to. He started pressurising me. I sent him one photo but he came back immediately. That wasn't what he wanted. He wanted something much more explicit – a photo of me in my underwear.

I was completely innocent. Not being at school meant I had missed out on sex education. In the books I'd read the sexual element was implied rather than explicitly detailed. I was very young in the head with regards to sexual relations, but it still felt wrong. I felt I had to do what he said, though. When I didn't respond he called me. He spoke so confidently and smoothly, as if this was the most normal thing in the world and it was me who was being weird and difficult by not sending him what he wanted.

It felt wrong and strange to do it, but I took a photo of myself in my underwear. Why would anyone want that? I didn't want to send it to him, but I felt like I had to because he was putting me under so much pressure. Reluctantly, I sent it. If I'd thought that was going to satisfy him, I was wrong. It only escalated further. He quickly demanded more pictures, even more explicit ones.

Next, he phoned me. 'Guess what I'm doing right this moment,' he said. I had no idea. I couldn't even begin to imagine.

The idea of relationships was confusing for me. I had a skewed idea of what one should be like because my brain is wired in a very strange way. I just don't know what is normal and what is not. I felt I had no option but to keep sending provocative photographs over text to him.

This type of correspondence went on for quite a while. I kept it secret, though. I wasn't sure what would happen if I told anyone. Then one day he phoned me: 'I'm coming to Brecon. I want you to meet me.'

Now I was scared. I had felt almost detached from it before, conducting things over the phone, but meeting up would suddenly make it real. Brecon was 30 miles away, so it would take some effort for me to get there.

'Come and meet me,' he persisted. 'I'll get the bed ready.'

That was it. It hit me in the face then. *I can't do that*, I thought. I was scared. I still didn't know what to do. All I knew was that I wanted it all to stop. I couldn't think of what else to do, so I threw my phone in the bin. My parents thought it strange that I had lost my phone, but I refused to let them in on the real story. I was quite shaken by the whole experience, and it made me question his motives. Was he really a genuine psychic or was it all a sham? I suspect it was the latter.

The episode with Phil came at a terrible time, when I was full of self-loathing and wasting away physically. I was starving myself. My health really deteriorated. I had little-to-no energy, but I would still push myself to exercise for hours at a time. My hair started falling out and my nails stopped growing. My periods became very irregular and eventually stopped altogether. I started getting spots and my hair was always greasy. At my lowest points, as well as cutting myself, I'd pull out clumps of hair.

Despite my physical and mental torment, I felt like I was achieving. I felt in control, like I was doing what I was supposed to do. It might sound strange, but I felt happiness at the suffering and pain, because I thought, *You can't get what you want or be happy unless you go through pain*.

For my mum and dad it was torture. They just couldn't understand why I would do this to myself. They continued to take me to see my psychiatrist. He kept pushing me to take antidepressants. I confided in him about my need to self-harm. He took out a toy doll and said, 'Pull the hair out of this.'

I looked at him like he was mad. How was that the same as pulling your own hair out?

'Put tomato ketchup on your legs,' he said, in response to the scars I was making. How could I compare the two? Self-harming was a pain I was willing to endure to take my mind off other things. The idea of putting ketchup on my leg just sounded strange. I just thought about how sticky I'd get, which repulsed me.

I was developing obsessive-compulsive disorder, and had started to value cleanliness above nearly everything else. The thought of willingly smearing ketchup on my legs was a no-no. Among my many daily rituals was obsessive hand-washing. I washed them over and over in the hottest water to kill the germs, until my hands were red. I had other rituals too, like doing specific hand movements a certain number of times. I'd turn around a certain number of times too, because I believed that if I didn't do it something bad would happen. I lay awake half the night doing hand gestures over and over again, because if I didn't do them 300 times I was certain something really bad was going to happen. There had been nothing to spark this. It was just something I had convinced myself of.

My OCD feels like something that has always been there. I can't remember how or when it started. I just always had to do things. In the 1990s the condition, like Asperger's, wasn't that understood. In rural Wales there just wasn't the health-care provision to advise on it.

In the grip of this mental maelstrom, my weight plummeted. I was down to six stone. My clothes hung off my skeletal shoulders. It became deadly serious then. The psychiatrist was clear about what action was needed.

'Sophie, you have a stark choice to make,' he told me. 'You can either stop dancing and go on antidepressants, or go to a psychiatric hospital where they will look after you.'

The thought of going to hospital terrified me. It was no choice, really. Reluctantly, I agreed to the medication. He prescribed the antidepressant fluoxetine, known more commonly as Prozac, for my desperately low mood, and diazepam, or Valium, for the anxiety. Despite my age, they prescribed a high dosage because my situation was so serious. We were at the point where they needed to do something or there was a risk I could do something really stupid.

The medication had an immediate effect. My mood lifted and I felt less inclined to cut myself, and with the edge taken off my anxiety, everyday things seemed less stressful. For the first time I thought I could go out, and that was a big deal. I went to the pharmacy by myself and, although it sounds like such a small thing, to someone who had effectively been locked inside all her life it was massive. It was like climbing Mount Everest.

As I'd done before when I'd been feeling depressed, I tried to articulate my feelings in poetry. One from that time was called 'My Time Is Now'.

My time for living is now.
I will no longer sleep,
As I have awakened from my long-lasting
   slumber.

It is too late to turn back.
The gate has closed.
My path is fixed.

Now out into the world I go!
With a smile on my face and love in my heart.
From my love I must depart.

Save your tears.
Do not cry.
Look into your memories for comfort from me.
Do not weep for you see I am already gone.

It was still a struggle, as those words demonstrate, but slowly I was engaging with the world around me. I could walk in the park near my house, go down into the town centre. By this point I was 16 and only beginning to sample things that everyone else took for granted.

The more my mood lifted, the more I wanted to meet people, so I looked to see if there were groups I could join. After years locked in my private universe, I was venturing out into the real world. What I didn't know was that evil was waiting.

Chapter 5

Tesco supermarket, Aberdare, May 2010

It's hard to believe that a seemingly innocent trip to a supermarket could have such devastating consequences. But that was how it was for me. I had no idea when I left the house on that mild May morning to go for a walk that I was inadvertently being led towards a dark path.

I exited the Aberdare Tesco store to see two Socialist Party activists handing out leaflets, trying to drum up support for their cause. I can't even remember what cause it was. I suspect it was highlighting the violence in Iraq – earlier that month the war-torn country had suffered its bloodiest day for six months as the power vacuum left by the military action to topple Saddam Hussein allowed terrorist groups like Al-Qaeda to flourish.

The two women stopped me. 'What are your views on war? Are you happy about the violence that comes from military action carried out in your name?' one said.

'Do you want to learn more? Come and join us and make a difference,' said the other.

One of them – an older American called Natalie – was very forthright. Their passion impressed me and their anti-war stance appealed to my inner pacifist activist. The other was called Susan, and she was more aloof.

They invited me to their next meeting. *Why not*, I thought. *What's the worst that could happen?*

If only I'd known.

The seeds for my decision to agree to their invitation had been sown a year earlier, when I'd had my first taste of political activism. Since taking the medication I had felt a lot better. I found it easier to go out alone and I was a lot happier in myself, but now, in retrospect, I can see the drugs clouded my thinking. I can't fathom why my mind does the things it does. Having Asperger's means I think logically and like to know what's coming. Yet one aspect of being bipolar was that I sometimes acted spontaneously, and under the influence of the medication it was this side that came to the fore.

I'd felt confident enough to start meeting new people. I wanted to engage with society for the first time. Plaid Cymru, the party for Welsh independence, had been canvassing in Aberdare and, as a bit of a Welsh nationalist,

I was keen to learn more. They held meetings in the town and I was up for going along. My dad came with me to the first few meetings and saw they were really nice people. My parents didn't have any particular political leaning towards the party, but they trusted me with them because their members were all older academics and it seemed I was in good care. When Dad then left me it felt good to be actually doing something on my own for the first time in my life. There would only be about ten people at the meetings, some were Mensa members, and the conversation was stimulating, the atmosphere relaxed.

I was happy there, but the drugs I was on made me feel quite high, like I could cope with anything. I felt like a different Sophie, one who didn't have to shy away from other people or get nervous about new things. I had turned 17 and I felt bolder.

So when I bumped into the Socialist Party activists they immediately appealed to me. They seemed younger, less academic, more vibrant and radical than the nationalists, more in your face. After being isolated for so long I was keen to see new things and meet new people.

A few days later I met up with them in the Tesco café. I still felt a bit intimidated by Natalie. She was in her fifties, tall and skinny and quite manly. She talked with great enthusiasm about the party and what they wanted to achieve.

'I'll think about it,' I said, and made to leave.

'Let me give you a lift,' Natalie said.

Before I could argue, we were driving back to my house.

'I want to meet your folks,' she said.

'I'm not sure that's a good idea,' I said, but she wasn't taking no for an answer.

My dad was quite bemused when I turned up with this radical American woman who launched into a diatribe about feminism on his doorstep.

A week later I went to their next meeting, held in a rundown room upstairs at a pub in Pontypridd, the town where my strange tutor had lived. There were about ten people there, and some of them were also rather strange. There was a man called Martin who made inappropriate comments on bestiality and such like.

'Don't mind him,' Natalie said. 'That's just what he's like. Don't take him seriously.'

They were all a lot older than me, but the average age was about 30, rather than the pensioner age of Plaid Cymru. Everyone addressed each other as 'comrade' and the topics of discussion were very earnest. There was obviously a deep-seated hatred of capitalism and the poll tax was still a running sore, and there was chat about Karl Marx and other communist things.

Natalie took an instant liking to me. She was quite the man-hater, as my dad had suspected, and I got the feeling she was gay. She was kind and considerate towards me from the off. Originally from Chicago, she had been living in Wales for many years and said she used to be a female miner. She was so thin that I wondered if she had an eating disorder.

I still had my own issues with food. As anyone who has suffered from an eating disorder knows, you never truly recover from it. It's always there, lurking in your psyche. I didn't let on about the issues I had, and I kept my Asperger's secret. I didn't want anyone thinking there was anything wrong with me. I wanted people to think I was normal. Maybe Natalie picked up on there being something strange about me, or maybe she just felt a strong mothering instinct. But she definitely took me under her wing, introducing me to everyone and making sure I ate snacks and had something to drink.

I liked the vibe of the meeting and resolved to go back. At the time I didn't have much else going on in my life. My schoolwork had fallen by the wayside. Once I'd turned 16 the local authority were no longer obliged to provide tutors for me, and I'd got the sense they were glad to see the back of me. As I'd only been having an hour a day's teaching, I hadn't covered enough of the curriculum to sit my GCSEs. There was the possibility of doing some kind of access course in the future, but at that moment I was in limbo. I didn't have my dance classes any longer and the spiritual church I'd gone to had closed down due to lack of numbers. I was at a loose end.

I turned my back on the nationalists – my parents didn't want me to leave Plaid Cymru, though, as at last they'd seen me settled within a group – and went along to more socialist meetings, where Natalie continued to look out for me. She was obsessed with making sure I ate enough. I was still very thin. She took pity on me and gave me money. I sensed this was causing some friction in the party. Natalie clearly carried some sway with the others and the presence of a new girl was leading to some mutterings of 'favouritism', particularly from Susan, the other woman I'd met outside Tesco. This was exacerbated when Natalie invited me to go to London with her to a socialist convention.

I was very anxious about going to such a big city, but Natalie paid for me to go, picked me up outside my house and sat with me on the bus from Cardiff that the party had organised to take us there. I started to get a little excited because I was finally going to get out of Wales and see some of London. The convention was on the outskirts of the city, however. It was very serious, and when it was over we got back on the bus and drove back to Cardiff. There was no chance of doing any sightseeing, but it was a good experience for me. I was coming out of my shell.

I had been with the party for four weeks when Susan invited me out canvassing with her in Aberaman, a small village south of Aberdare. We went from door to door, trying to speak to people about our cause. She did all of the talking. I just stood there, handing out the leaflets – when anyone gave us a chance, that is. It was a dispiriting experience. Most people just said, 'Not today, thank you,' and that was when they were being polite. Some just swore at us and slammed the door.

We had been at it all day. My feet were killing and I was fit to drop.

'I want to go home,' I said to Susan, after the latest door had closed in our faces.

'Just one more,' she said. We were in the middle of a seemingly neverending street of small terraced houses.

I reluctantly agreed. One more couldn't hurt, could it? We went up and knocked on the door. For a moment I didn't think anyone was coming.

'Let's go,' I said.

Then the door opened. A man in a white vest and baggy jeans filled the doorframe. He must have been six-foot plus, with broad shoulders and cropped black hair.

'Hi, how are you?' Susan said, launching into her spiel about the socialists. I was half turning on my heel, just waiting for the cue to leave.

'Oh, right,' he said, in a well-spoken English accent. 'You'd better come in, then.'

I couldn't believe it. I just wanted to go home.

He ushered us through to a neatly furnished sitting room. The television was on with the sound down. The smell of cooking wafted in from the kitchen. He appeared to be living with an elderly couple. I perched on the edge of a small sofa. Susan was trying to show him the literature, but he just sat looking directly at me the whole time and smiling. I felt a bit uncomfortable but I didn't say anything.

'So if you're interested, come along,' Susan was saying. 'We're always looking for new members.'

The man continued to stare, like he was examining me.

'I will be there,' he said, smiling as he showed us outside again.

Relieved, all I could think about was being home in a few minutes' time. As we walked away I glanced back to see him still standing there, staring. I felt a little strange, but Susan was in high spirits, as she had a potential new member of the party, so I put the feeling out of my head. I turned away, not thinking much more about it – and not realising for one moment that with that one brief encounter my fate was sealed.

Chapter 6

It's weird how things happen. I often think that, about a lot of events, but it was particularly true of that time. It was like I was at the mercy of cruel fate.

By the time the next socialist meeting arrived things had changed. Natalie, my mentor, had left. She'd gone back to America. It was so sudden. She had been my reason for going along to the meetings, the one who looked after me, who was showing me so much about the world I had entered. Now she was gone. It upset me. She'd never said a word that she might be leaving. Maybe if she had been there things would have been different. She might have sensed danger and protected me. Instead, I was on my own.

At the next meeting he was there. Maybe I shouldn't have been surprised. I was no sooner in the door than he made a beeline for me.

'Hello again,' he said, smiling. He didn't look as imposing as he had the week before. He was a lot smarter: clean-shaven, in a pressed shirt and smelling strongly of aftershave. He told me his name. It is too painful for me to recount. Just the mention of it conjures up images too terrifying to contemplate. So for the purposes of this book I just want to refer to him as 'ST'. To call him by his name humanises something that isn't human.

He was full of questions. How long had I been in the Socialist Party? What made me join? He spoke with the deepest voice. He sounded sophisticated and intelligent – posh, some people might say.

'How old are you?' he said.

'Seventeen.'

'Oh,' he said, looking me up and down. 'You look much older than seventeen.'

I didn't. The opposite was true. I looked about twelve.

The meeting began and I didn't think too much about him, but during a break he approached and bumped into me. His hand brushed mine. He started talking about cats and how much he loved them. By this time we had cats and I loved animals in general, so that caught my interest. He asked me about mine and seemed genuinely interested, smiling and nodding and chatting away. He was very smiley and talkative. He reminded me of a big child – very excitable, like this was the most interesting thing in the world. I watched, quite intrigued, as I was always morose and quiet. I saw how people reacted to him and largely it was positive. Only Jonathan, a man who'd been quite friendly towards me, seemed to be eyeing him suspiciously. I didn't read much into it, though.

The meeting continued, and when there was another break ST came up and grabbed my hand.

'Sorry,' he said, like it had been an accident.

He started chatting again and asked me where I was from, so I told him it was Aberdare. It all seemed innocuous. I didn't really think too much about him, but a couple of days later I was in the town centre, walking past a card shop, and he literally jumped out at me, nearly knocking me over. He grabbed my hand again, as if by accident. We chatted for a bit and went our separate ways. I put it down to coincidence. A day or so later my mum said to me, 'Sophie, there's a man standing in the street looking at the house. Do you know anything about him?'

I looked out but there was nobody there.

'That's strange,' Mum said. 'He just seemed to be loitering out there.'

I shrugged and went back to what I was doing.

The following day there was a knock at the door. My mum answered to find a man standing there holding two Magnum ice creams. She didn't know who he was and her instinct was to tell him to go away, but she called me. It was ST, standing there, all in white. I was shocked to see him but I didn't show it, as he had a big smile on his face.

'Hi,' he said, beaming and holding one of the ice creams out towards me. 'It's such a lovely day, isn't it? Want to come with me to the park?'

Who was this person, I thought, who kept popping up everywhere? How did he know where I lived? For someone more experienced, this might have set alarm bells ringing. But I didn't know what to think.

'Come on, it's not a day to be indoors. Come over to the park with me.' He was still holding out the ice cream. 'Take it, before it melts.'

It was a sunny day. The ice cream looked inviting. Before I knew what was happening he had grabbed my hand and I was walking with him down the street, eating the Magnum. All the time I kept thinking, *Is this what normal people do?* He looked so relaxed and confident, as if this was something people did all the time. I was beyond naïve. It was still only a matter of weeks since I'd joined the socialists and I had so little experience of human behaviour, and what I did possess was seen through the prism of Asperger's and medication.

I felt a bit intimidated and wasn't sure what to say. Near my house was a large, beautifully preserved Victorian park with a road around it where motorbike races were held in summer, and we headed there. I asked him how old he was. He said he was 30, which meant there were 13 years between us. That seemed like a big age gap, but he acted as though it wasn't a big deal. Maybe it wasn't, I thought.

As we walked he talked a lot about himself and asked me lots of questions. I asked him how he knew where I lived. He avoided the question and just kept talking about other things. He was so full-on that my head spun just listening to him. He seemed to be offering up lots of information. The people he lived with were his elderly former foster parents, David and Margaret. He was originally from Slough, in Berkshire, and had been in care as a young boy but was still close to his mum, who lived not far from him in Wales. He told me he used to be a manager of a computer shop in Merthyr Tydfil but was currently out of work and getting by on money loaned to him by David and Margaret and whatever he got from Jobseeker's Allowance. He talked about computers and was so animated that it almost made me breathless. He said he liked to wear white as it made him feel 'godly', whatever that meant. He seemed happy all the time – the complete opposite to me.

When he asked about my life I felt I could tell him about my own issues. I talked about having Asperger's and the medication I was on. Maybe I shared too much, but I had no filter and he seemed genuinely interested. I told him about my anxieties, the outbursts I'd had and the way people treated me. I opened up about having to leave school and my dance teacher and how all these damaging experiences had made me feel. The only people I'd really spoken to about these sorts of things before were healthcare professionals. I also told him about the things I liked – the causes I felt strongly about, like being anti-war, and the movies and books I liked.

He talked about his love of animals. He spoke movingly about a cat belonging to his foster mother that had died from cancer. It seemed to have affected him quite seriously, and this resonated with me deeply. I had always been a passionate lover of animals. I told him about my campaigning for animal rights and he seemed to really care. I hadn't met many people in my life, but here was someone who seemed to share my passion. I told him I was a vegetarian and he said he was trying to stop eating meat too.

When I mentioned my views on television and how I thought it was a form of brainwashing, he agreed. It seemed to set him off on something, as he went on about secret sects and mind control. He was into conspiracy theories. He talked about wealth, power, the New World Order and the Illuminati, and how the planet was run by a secret sect. I had never heard anyone speak like that before. It seemed fanciful but he believed it. He said he listened to Alex Jones of infowars.com and David Icke, the former BBC presenter turned conspiracy theorist. He said he thought we were being ruled by a group of people who engaged in ritualistic sacrifice and wanted to kill us with 'chemtrails' from high-flying planes and 'put things in the water and our food to control us'.

As we walked he kept brushing his hand against mine. Then he held it, quite tightly. He was so close to me, pulling me in towards him. All the time I questioned whether this was normal behaviour. I had seen other people doing it so maybe it was.

I was confused. On the one hand it was nice to have someone to talk to. He was outgoing and confident and so unlike anyone else I'd ever met – not that I had a whole host of people to compare him to. But on the other hand, something didn't feel right. Maybe if I hadn't been on medication I'd have reacted differently. My anxiety might have taken over. Still on a high from my newfound confidence, however, I felt I was ready for anything.

When I got home my parents wanted to know who this man was. I told them I'd met him through the party. They had concerns because he was so much older than me. I didn't know what to say. I didn't want anyone to think I couldn't handle it myself. I thought I was a grown-up and I could deal with it.

At the next socialist meeting he latched on to me immediately again. Everybody else seemed to like him. He had a persona that people responded to, but he practically moved me away from other members so they couldn't speak to me. Without Natalie there I didn't really have a close friend, but he was taking such a keen interest it would have been hard for anyone to get a word in. He was persistent about me coming to his house. I still wasn't sure. Something told me this wasn't right.

A day or so later he arrived at my door again. He seemed interested in the number of cats that hung around our house. I explained that they were strays my family fed. My mother has always liked to feed stray cats and the garden birds, and we also have hedgehogs that come for food. My parents officially only had one cat, called Faith, but my mum fed a number of strays that came to the house and sort of adopted them. One moggy we called Baby had been coming for years so was practically ours. ST made a fuss of the cats and again it impressed me that he was kind to animals.

I told him about our other animals. We had adopted an abused rabbit and nursed him back to health and also rescued two guinea pigs. Our beloved Dalmatian, Ben, had died a few years earlier, and my parents had since got two other dogs, Angel and Sammy, who were springer spaniels. He told me that when he was young he had a dog who went everywhere with him and used to sleep on his bed. He said the dog was like his best friend. I asked him what breed the dog was and what its name was. He seemed keen to change the subject, which I found a little odd given how enthusiastic he had been about all things to do with animals, but I didn't think much more about it.

My parents wanted to know who this man was who was showing such a keen interest in their daughter, so I took him inside to meet them. I was quite tense, wondering how it would play out. He chatted away, like I had seen him doing with the socialists. I could sense Dad was eyeing him suspiciously. Mum was quite chatty to him. Later, she told me she had been worried about the age gap from the outset and had revealed her concerns to her hairdresser, who told her, 'As long as he treats her right, age makes no difference.' So she tried to look past it.

He only stayed talking to them for a few minutes before suggesting we go out for a walk in the woods. How could I say no? It was like I couldn't find the words. He was so persuasive. I felt like I was in a dream – not because I was walking on air with happiness, but because I was being led, trance-like, with no control over my actions.

As we walked he made a comment about my father's attitude. He could tell by Dad's body language that he didn't like him. I was confused. I suspected he was right and that Dad didn't like him, but I also knew that Dad would only be trying to protect me. From what, though? The simple fact was that they hadn't told me I couldn't spend time with him. And even if they had, I wasn't sure how I would have reacted.

We continued walking and he held my hand tightly and pulled me close to him. Not in any romantic way – it was more possessive. My heart was beating really fast and my head was spinning.

I had no understanding of what a relationship was like. Did people not go on dates – to the cinema, or a café or restaurant? Was it not more formal and slower than this? However, as we walked and chatted more about our lives, he made me feel like he was listening to my grievances. He came across as sympathetic and understanding.

'You should definitely come back to my place,' he said again. 'We'll watch a film together. It'll be fun.'

The way he said it made it sound as though it would be fun. Maybe this was what people did. They hung out together and watched films and chatted. I'd never had a friend before. Maybe it would be good for me. It was 6 p.m. and it wasn't as though I was doing anything else.

'Come on,' he said. 'We can watch *The Nightmare Before Christmas*.'

The Tim Burton film was one of my favourites. Had I told him that previously? I couldn't remember. As we drove to Aberaman in his old red banger of a car I recalled the house where I'd first met this man – the smell of cooking and the homely atmosphere. It might not be so bad to hang out there, I thought. It had only been three weeks since that encounter, but it seemed longer, like I had known him for ages. He pulled up at the house and we went inside. David and Margaret were there. She offered a tight smile but he just glared. ST didn't show me into the living room but instead ushered me upstairs to a small bedroom. It was a bit messy. I became twitchy. This wasn't good for my OCD. Aside from the bed and the chest of drawers with a television on top, the room was strewn with weight-lifting equipment and muscle-bulking supplements. Again, I wondered if these things were normal for a man to have.

The only place to sit was his airbed, so I perched while he played around with the TV and put the movie on. I didn't feel comfortable at all, but I tried to focus on the movie when it began. I'd loved the stop-motion animation the first time I saw it and the dark fantasy element reminded me of *The Dark Crystal*. Something in me related to Sally, the ragdoll character whose attempts to bring Christmas spirit to spooky Halloween Town are doomed.

It was a summer evening and he drew the curtains, extinguishing all light save for the flickering screen. He sat right next to me on the bed. I shifted over slightly, as he was pressing against me, but he slid further over. I had issues with personal space and felt claustrophobic in tight spaces, but I didn't say anything. He held my hand with one hand and put his other arm around me, pulling me into his large frame.

My breathing increased and my body tensed. For what? I had no idea. We watched the film, his grip never loosening. I sat rigid. Instinct told me something was not right, but I couldn't work out what.

He pulled me towards him and kissed me on the lips. It was forceful and yukky. This was my first kiss, but wasn't it supposed to be tender, enjoyable? Was he even my boyfriend? What did this mean?

Without a word of warning he pushed me back onto the airbed. I put my hand up against him in protest. I couldn't find my voice.

'Don't worry,' he said. He was breathing more heavily. I could feel it on my face. *No*, I thought. *No*. This wasn't right. I didn't want this. His hands were everywhere but this wasn't gentle caressing. I felt no sense of affection. It was purposeful. He tore at my clothes. I was helpless. I tried to stop him but he just kept saying, 'Don't worry. It'll be fine. You'll like it.'

My head was spinning. He pushed himself on top of me, squeezing the air from my lungs. He was panting now, in my face. He pinned me down, removing every bit of clothing from both of us. No, I tried to say, but he was choking the breath from me. I felt him wriggle for position, and then it happened.

An explosion of pain. That's the only way I can describe it. I thought my insides were being ripped apart. I'd never known agonising pain like it. He was pushing harder and harder, the bed felt like a block of concrete behind my head. I wanted to scream in pain but I didn't have the breath. I wanted to shout out but I had no words. On and on it went. I thought of David and Margaret downstairs. Would they not hear what was going on? Would they come and investigate?

And then he stopped. He had got what he wanted. But for me the agony went on. He rolled over but kept me in his iron grip. I wanted to cry but I couldn't move. All I could do was lie there in an inferno of suffering and wonder what had just happened to me – and why. I was aware of the movie still flickering on the TV screen, lighting up the walls with ghastly shapes.

He held me for a long time afterwards. Not in a loving embrace, but rather like how a lion protects a fresh kill. I tried to process what had just happened. We'd had sex. I understood that. My first time. I hadn't given much thought to how it might happen. I realised people did it and it was part of growing up, but I thought there might have been some build-up, some expectation, longing even. In my naïve mind I thought people in a relation-ship built towards that special moment when their union was consummated. I thought there might have been some sort of courtship – some gentle kissing, some tentative fumbling and then an understanding that the act was going to take place.

I must have been mistaken. It wasn't like that at all. There was no warning, no time to prepare. He just took what he considered to be his. I felt violated – it wasn't consensual. I hadn't wanted it. I'd tried to fend him off but he'd moved so quickly and decisively I'd been completely powerless to stop him. It had all happened so fast. I started to think then about the implications.

'Did you use any protection?' I said, when I finally found my voice.

'No. I'm against it. It puts me off.'

Okay. So if he didn't use protection then what was stopping me becoming pregnant? The thought scared me. I could barely look after myself. What would I do if I had to bring a baby into this world? Oh God. The consequences didn't bear thinking about.

'Are you okay?' he said.

I wasn't sure but I thought I should nod.

'I've been wanting to do that since the first time I set eyes on you,' he said. 'I don't think I could live without you.'

I just lay there, mind still whirring.

After a while he said he would take me home. We walked downstairs, where David and Margaret were looking at me. It took all my strength to smile and pretend everything was fine, while inside I felt so terribly shaky and anxious. I kept my feelings hidden. They were just an elderly couple. I didn't want to worry them.

Eventually, he drove me home. He was so calm about everything. When he dropped me off at my house I went in feeling sore, strange and confused. All that kept going through my mind was, *Is this normal?*

Was this all just part of growing up? I knew I was very socially naïve and couldn't read people very well. Maybe I had missed the signs. Perhaps it had been obvious what was about to happen and I hadn't realised.

As I climbed into bed it struck me that we hadn't even watched the movie – the reason he'd asked me back to his place. It was hard not to think that was somehow darkly appropriate. Was I entering my own nightmare?

Chapter 7

That night I didn't sleep a wink. He was texting me all the time: 'It's okay, it's normal, don't worry.'

I had no friends to confide in, and there was no way I could tell my parents what had happened, so there was no one to ask if I should be worried. I would have been too embarrassed to speak to someone anyway. I felt so shameful, like somehow this was all my own fault. All I had was his reassurance. Maybe I was overreacting. Maybe it was normal and it would all be fine.

My head was spinning, though. It had all happened so fast. He made it seem like he had known me forever, but the reality was that we had only spent a few days in each other's company. I had gone from not knowing him at all to knowing him. It was very confusing, and I didn't know how to respond. I didn't have the experience to deal with this.

And then there was the lack of protection. I might have been naïve but I knew enough to understand that there was a danger I could get pregnant. That freaked me out. I lay awake sweating. What was going to happen to me?

In the morning he pestered me to meet up. It was like I couldn't say no. My parents probed me for information about where we had been. I couldn't bear their questioning so I just shut them down. When he appeared at our doorstep I told my parents I was going out. They tried to intervene. For them it must have been odd. Here was their daughter, someone who rarely went out, but now she was going out again with an older man who they knew hardly anything about.

We went for a walk and he was sympathetic. He listened as I tried to explain why this was a strange experience for me because of the kind of life I'd had.

'Your parents don't really understand you,' he said. 'They don't want you to grow up. They are trying to control you. You're better off with me looking after you.'

The way he spoke, it was like he was picking up on my secret thoughts – like he was right. Maybe my parents were just trying to keep me in a box. I was still on medication and it was bolstering my opinion that I could handle myself.

I told him I was worried about the lack of protection.

'It's okay,' he said. 'If you want, we can go to the pharmacy and get you a morning-after pill.'

I didn't know what that was. He explained that it was a fail-safe for girls who weren't taking the contraceptive pill.

'I think we should do that,' I said.

He was not like the man who had been so violent the night before. This was the gentler man who had been so full on. We went to a chemist in Aberdare. The woman behind the counter looked at us both suspiciously, like she could tell something was up.

'How old are you?' she said. I thought she was talking to me, but she was addressing him.

'What's it got to do with you?' he snapped.

'I need to establish a few things first,' she said.

'Why did you not use contraception?' She was really having a go at him.

He switched in an instant and started getting angry. He started accusing her of prying and stormed off. I caught the woman's eye. She was looking at me sympathetically. What did she suspect was going on?

I didn't know what to do at first, but I eventually ran after him and caught up with him along the street. He started ranting about who that woman thought she was. I was stunned that someone could get so worked up about a brief exchange. He soon calmed down and acted like nothing had happened. I just stood there, unsure what to say or do. In all the fuss I'd forgotten that I hadn't even managed to get the morning-after pill. After a few moments he said he wanted to go back to his foster parents' home. I feared what was coming, and once we were in his bedroom I tried to distract him by exploring the stuff lying around and asking lots of questions. I picked up a strange contraption.

'What's this?' I turned it over in my hands.

'That,' he said, taking it off me, 'is a penis stretcher.'

'Oh,' I said, thinking of what that meant. 'I don't think you should use that.'

He looked a bit self-conscious. 'I need it,' he said.

I couldn't understand why he would want something like that. But before I could think any more about it he had grabbed me and dragged me over to the bed. I knew what was coming. Like before, there was no way to stop it. He pinned me down and forced himself upon me. I went rigid with fear and braced myself until it was over and I could breathe again. Like the first time, this didn't feel loving or sensual. It was an animal act.

'You drive me wild,' he said. 'I've never felt this way about anyone before.'

I lay there in silence until he told me it was time to go downstairs. This time he took me into the living room, where Margaret and David were watching television. He sat down on the sofa and pulled me onto his lap, like a dad might do to his young daughter. I cringed with embarrassment and tried to pull my dress over my knees. He gripped me tightly.

'Would you like some tea, my dear?' Margaret said, not looking me in the eye. I think she felt embarrassed.

I nodded and tried to smile politely. 'Yes, please.'

David just sat there, staring at me. I tried to pull my clothing down further. It looked like he was staring up my dress. I wanted to move positions because I felt uncomfortable, but ST wouldn't let me. Every time I wriggled his grip tightened.

Margaret came back with a Victoria sponge cake. 'I made this for you, dear,' she said.

I tried my best to be grateful when all I wanted was to be as far away from this house as possible. Surely they must have known what he was doing to me. Margaret came back and made small talk, but I could sense her embarrassment. Was she concerned by how young I was? Did she know what he was like? As I watched her tiptoe around him I saw how tiny she was compared to his bulky frame, and I wondered how she would ever tell him to do anything.

On the way home he said he was going to have to move out. He said he had only moved there as a temporary measure but had stayed longer than he'd planned. Margaret had been diagnosed with cancer, and her grandson had spoken to ST about finding his own place so his grandmother didn't have another person to run around after. He had been onto the council about a new place.

He dropped me off at home and I walked inside feeling strange – like my mind was not my own. I felt completely confused and torn. I was desperate to be a stronger, more independent teenager but was slipping under the control of this man.

The next few days followed the same pattern. He would come for me, take me out, we'd walk and talk about our lives and then he'd take me to his house, where he would expect sex. He still occasionally wore his white clothes but sometimes he turned up in a T-shirt and jeans. One T-shirt he liked was orange with a cartoon figure on it with a large penis, above which was written 'Big Man'. I thought it was disgusting, but when I said I felt it was in bad taste and embarrassing he just laughed. Now when he talked it was less upbeat and boyish. He didn't talk too much specifically about his own life, but he liked to big himself up, bragging about how intelligent he was. I wasn't sure if this was in an effort to impress me.

In contrast, I found myself telling him about the books I loved to read, how I collected dolls and what my home life was like. I gave more details about my anxieties – the types of things that used to terrify me as a youngster, from going to the cinema to even the thought of using a public toilet. That was something I never did, because of my germ phobia and because being inside a cubicle brought on feelings of claustrophobia.

I'd never had this opportunity before. I'd never met someone actually interested in what I thought about things. Growing up, not having any friends to confide in or share stories with, I must have been bottling everything up. And now, perhaps buoyed by the medication I was taking, the floodgates were opening. And what's more, he encouraged me to talk, he listened to everything I said and seemed genuinely concerned, shocked and sympathetic. For the first time in my life I opened up about my eating disorder, self-harm, OCD and my depression, and the effect they'd had on me. I also told him about my dad's illness and what a struggle it had been for my mum and him. It was like a great weight was being lifted from my shoulders. It was a revelation.

But there were other factors at work – which I didn't appreciate fully at the time. For a child with severe mental illness who had never been around people apart from my family in my whole life, it was impossible to know how to act socially. Everything was going very fast and he was pushing.

He must have known I was vulnerable and, although he made me feel uncomfortable, the fact that he listened and paid me many compliments had an overwhelming effect. He kept telling me he was the only person I could trust in the whole world.

'Everyone else will just let you down or lie to you,' he said. 'But not me.'

He made me feel like we were a couple – like he was my boyfriend. He kissed me and held my hand. This didn't make sense to me. I was so confused.

He was charming yet very obsessive and demanding. I thought that was normal and okay. When he talked about my family he would put little jibes in here and there, and he got me to believe that he was the only one who cared about me – that my family wanted to stop me from being happy. He was constantly dripping poison in my ears about them. At first what he said sounded wrong, but whenever I came home and my parents started questioning me, I thought, *Maybe he is right*.

My family were getting concerned about the amount of time we were spending together. This was a new thing for me. I had seen them agitated and stressed over my behaviour before, but this was different. I never liked upsetting my family, so it was torture for me; I felt like I was being pulled in two different directions and, as he was the more persuasive and manipulative, he won.

Over a month after our first meeting he suggested we go for a walk in Cwm Cadlan, a nature reserve not far from Aberdare. We drove to a secluded spot and parked. I moved to get out of the car, but he stopped me and grabbed my arm.

He had a look in his eyes that I had only seen in his bedroom before.

'I love you, Sophie. I can't handle being apart from you. Do you love me too?'

What could I say? Was this love? It didn't feel like I thought it would.

'Do you? Tell me.' His grip tightened.

'Yes, of course.'

'Say it.'

'I do.' I felt my cheeks flush. It felt awkward and wrong.

'Say you love me.'

I paused, trying to work out the implications of what I was saying. 'I. Love. You,' I said, haltingly and quietly.

'I knew it.' His face lit up. He started to get agitated. 'I want to do it right here in the car,' he said.

What? In the open? In this rusty old banger of a car? So anyone could see? I looked around. There wasn't anybody I could see. It was getting late in the afternoon but that didn't mean we'd be alone. The place was popular with walkers. Anyone could stumble upon us. But that wasn't even the biggest issue. I didn't want to have sex with him. Not here, not ever. I just wanted to go home.

'I don't know …' I said. 'Can't you just take me home?'

He gripped me so tightly and manoeuvred me into the back of the car. Then he climbed on top of me, forcing me back into the seat. He was crushing me and grabbing me so violently that I heard my top rip and my bra strap break. It was like he was possessed. I braced myself for the pain that was coming, but he had other plans. He undid his trousers, but this time he grabbed my head and rammed it towards his crotch. I thought I was going to choke.

When it was over he still demanded his walk. It was starting to get dark and I didn't have a jumper or coat. Summer was fading fast and the nights were cold, particularly up there.

'Only a bit further,' he said. He seemed to be taking delight in my discomfort.

Time was getting on and I could imagine my parents at home worrying about me. I had never stayed out this late before and I hadn't told them where I was going or what time I'd be back. I didn't have any medication on me and it had gone past the time for my next dose. I began to get upset. I was desperate for the toilet, which did nothing to calm my anxiety.

'Please just take me home,' I pleaded. 'My parents will be wondering where I am.'

'Oh, yes,' he said. 'Your poor, sick dad. This will really be stressing him out.'

'I need to go to the toilet.'

'There are toilets here,' he said, knowing full well of my phobia.

'I can't use a public toilet.'

'Well, then, you're stuck.' He was definitely enjoying this.

The trauma of what can only be described as a sexual assault, the cold, the panic from not taking my medication, the knowledge that I was worrying my family. It was all too much.

We walked to the toilets. They were closed.

He laughed. 'I guess that solves that problem.'

'I just want to go home,' I said. I was freaking out now. We had been out half the night and I was utterly miserable.

'I'm sorry,' he said, his tone softening. 'It was an accident. Believe me. I didn't realise the time and I didn't think the toilets would be shut. I'll take you home.'

We drove towards the gates. I couldn't believe it – they were locked, and had been since 8 p.m. It was now nearly midnight.

'Ha! Now you have no choice but to spend the night with me here.' He laughed. It no longer seemed like an accident.

I started to panic. I was worried about how my parents would react, but I called them anyway. I had to.

'I'm so sorry,' I said. 'I'm stuck here.'

I could detect the concern in my mum's voice but also relief that at least we hadn't been in an accident. There was nothing they could do, though. They couldn't come and get me because the gates were closed.

He took the phone off me. 'Sophie's fine,' he said, sounding so reassuring and nice. 'There is nothing to worry about. I'm sorry. This was a genuine accident. We lost track of time. I'm looking after her. Nothing will happen. It was a genuine mistake, but I will keep her safe. And don't worry, we have food and drink in the car. Yes … the toilets are open.'

He was lying. We had nothing and the toilets were locked. My parents were still worried to death, but I think it put their minds at ease a little, hearing that he was in control of the situation.

I spent a miserable few hours shivering in his beat-up car, desperately trying to hold my urine in, my bladder in agony. All the time he was making out that it was some kind of romantic adventure. There was no way this was an accident. He must have known what time it was. We had to stay there until 9 a.m., when they opened the gates. We had been there since 3 p.m. the day before.

'Here,' he said, when we finally pulled up at my house. 'At last I got to spend the night with you.'

That convinced me he had planned it all along. When I finally got inside, my parents gave me a hug and asked how I was. I said I was fine, but it had really taken it out of me. I hadn't eaten or drunk anything for all that time. My tummy was still in agony. I could tell my parents thought something bad had happened to me.

That incident only hardened their opinion that this man was bad news. They told me to stop seeing him. Deep down I knew they were right, but when he texted or called or turned up in his car I felt I had to do what he said. My mind couldn't rationalise what I was doing.

After that night in the hills he was desperate to have sex in the back of the car. He looked for any opportunity. I was mortified – not only at having to do it repeatedly, but from the shame that someone might see us.

Then something happened that made me yearn for the times when that was all I had to feel ashamed about.

Wales is blessed with many mountains, and another popular spot near Abercynon is the Giant's Tooth viewpoint. It's a long walk to get there and the scenery is breathtaking. We had nearly reached the viewpoint and there was no one around. Without warning he pushed me to the ground, shoving my head into the dirt. Before I even had a chance to resist, he pulled my jeans and knickers down and had sex with me from behind. When he had finished he just got up and left me lying there, covered in dirt, my trousers by my ankles, feeling utterly violated.

I couldn't speak afterwards. I was in a state of shock. We went back to the car and he drove me home. Once he'd dropped me off he sped off. I couldn't face my family so I just walked past our house and kept going. I thought of people I hadn't spoken to for a long time. I had no friends as such, but there were some people I had been in touch with from the political parties and campaigns. I tried calling them on my mobile phone, even though I hadn't spoken to some of them for a long time. He didn't like me interacting with other people and had discouraged me from going to the party meetings. I didn't see it, but he was starting to isolate me from the only group I socialised with. I wasn't even sure what I would say to them. I just wanted to make a connection to someone, anyone. No one answered. I had never felt so lonely in my life before.

I went home eventually, avoided my parents and buried my head in my pillow, waiting for his inevitable text messages to buzz again.

When he next got in touch he acted like nothing had happened. In fact, he was in an especially happy mood. He showed off a set of keys – for a place of his own. It was in Penrhiwceiber, where my grandfather lived, but in a very rough area. It was a three-storey terraced house, and I could only assume that the reason he got it so quickly from the council was because no one else would touch it. He showed me into it proudly, but I had never seen a house in such a diabolical state before. There were no carpets, the entranceway was painted light purple with dark purple swirls going all around it, and the living room was painted bright green.

'I call this the Green Room,' he said proudly.

I looked around nervously for somewhere to sit. He had no furniture except for an airbed, so I sat on the floorboards. On the walls he'd written lots of strange things with a marker pen. I couldn't believe some of the things he had written – lots of awful fantasies about me and how he wanted me to have sex with lots of black men. There was even mention of me having sex with a horse. It was disgusting. Other scribbles were about rape, and he seemed fixated with large penises. I didn't want to keep reading, but I couldn't help noticing that he'd also written about the New World Order and the Illuminati and the types of things he had ranted about to me before. There were no curtains, so everyone passing could look in.

We had only been there for a matter of moments before he half-grabbed, half-lifted me onto the airbed.

'But people could see us,' I protested.

'So?'

He seemed to get a kick from the fact that it was broad daylight and anyone could see us. I lay like a ragdoll as he took off my clothes and tore off his own. He was becoming increasingly frenzied and violent, and now that he had his own place he was like an animal unleashed. He put both hands around my neck as he thrust into me. I put my hands up to push them off but I was no match for him. I tried to kick but he only seemed to get off on it more. He squeezed tighter. My mind went blank. I was about to pass out. I think I went limp because I can't remember what happened until it was over and I was lying in the empty room, shivering and shaking, my teeth chattering, my body blue, both from the cold and from where he had grabbed me.

He came back with something.

'Here, drink this,' he said. 'You'll like it.'

I didn't know what it was. He didn't tell me. I took it because my throat was burning and I was desperate for anything to soothe it. My mind was racing. Even in my confused state I knew that this was not normal. People in a relationship did not violently strangle their partners. I felt so scared. I was too frightened even to go home. My parents had been right: I should stay away from this man. I felt shame and confusion and guilt that I had put myself in this position.

The drink gave me a warm glow. My head felt fuzzy. I wasn't sure what was happening to me. I just felt very tired and not entirely in control of my senses.

When I woke up I was still shivering and my head was throbbing. It was dark outside but the streetlights poured into the room. I was lying on the floor. I sat up and saw that he was in bed with a cover over him. What time was it? I should have been home. Then I remembered what had happened earlier and why I hadn't wanted to face my parents. I cuddled my knees into me to try to keep warm and prayed dawn would be here soon.

'You were out of it last night,' he said, almost triumphantly, when he finally woke up in the morning.

'What happened?'

'You were drunk.'

'Drunk?' I had never tasted alcohol in my life before. With the high doses of medication I was on, I was strongly advised not to touch the stuff.

'Blitzed,' he laughed.

'I don't remember,' I said, rubbing my head. How much had I had? What even was it that I'd drunk anyway?

'What? You can't remember a thing?' he said. 'Not even our mind-blowing sex?'

What was he saying? Had I been so out of it that he'd had sex with me without my realising? My body ached so much that I couldn't tell if it had been from his violent attack before.

'And do you not remember me kicking you out of bed?' He was grinning.

I shook my head.

'Your feet were bloody freezing. Like ice blocks. So I kicked you out. You can sleep on the floor in future.'

I looked out of the window and saw people walking by, looking in. I suddenly realised I was still naked. What had people seen?

As recently as a year ago I hadn't been able to get through the night without my mum lying next to me. Now I was in the bed of a man I hardly knew. Well, I wasn't even in the bed. A man, who just a few weeks previously had been a stranger, was kicking me out of his bed. Why was this happening to me?

I had to tell him I didn't want to do this anymore. We got dressed and I looked at my reflection in his bathroom mirror. I looked terrible. My parents were going to kill me. As we were getting ready for him to take me home I decided this was it.

'I don't think we should see each other anymore,' I said.

'What?' He wasn't smiling now. 'Are you leaving me, Sophie?' There was a tone to his voice that I hadn't heard before. 'I don't think you realise what you're saying. We're together now, Sophie. We love each other. You told me, remember. We'll always be together, you and I. We're going to be joined at the hip. Nothing is coming between us.'

I stared blankly. I didn't know what to say.

He started scrambling around, looking for something. He found a DVD and put it on. It was the animated Disney movie *Aladdin*. 'Look,' he said, fast-forwarding it to the scene where Aladdin takes Princess Jasmine on a magic carpet ride to the song 'A Whole New World'. 'This is us. I'm Aladdin and you're Jasmine.'

He made me watch while he sang along and encouraged me to join in. I knew the song, but now hearing the words about showing me the world, opening my eyes and there being no one to tell us no, it seemed to take on a new, darker meaning.

'Aren't the words amazing?' he said, his eyes lit up like

a child's, or perhaps someone, I could imagine, on drugs. 'I'll call you Jasmine and you should call me Aladdin. You must learn these words so we can sing it together.'

He was serious. This was so strange. One moment he scared me with his violence, the next he was overbearing with his affection. Surely this couldn't be what relationships were like?

His voice then took on a different tone. 'And you wouldn't want to try to leave me, would you?' He was looking directly into my eyes. 'Think of how fragile your father is, Sophie. It wouldn't take much to send him over the edge now, would it? If anything happened to split us up, I could easily see him going downhill very fast.'

Shivers went down my spine. He was still staring at me, but there was no light in his eyes.

'What do you mean?' I said, shaking, scared of what the answer might be.

He shrugged. 'All I'm saying is that it would be easy to fuck him up. How do you think he would like to hear what you're like? What you're into?'

'What?'

'How sex mad you are? How much you like it? What do you think that would do to his health, imagining all these things about his little-princess baby daughter?'

He couldn't be serious. Why would he tell my dad what he did to me – and twist it in such a vile way? I thought of my parents. We were not what you would call sexually liberated people. We were the type of family that fast-forwarded sex scenes in movies. If he did tell them what we had been doing, the shock might well kill my dad, particularly given how ill he had been.

'You wouldn't do that,' I said.

'Wouldn't I? You have no idea what I would and wouldn't do.' He pulled me so close that the only thing I could inhale was his foul breath. 'I've told you I love you – more than life itself. We are going to be together forever and I'll do whatever it takes to make sure it happens. We will never be apart. I'll kill anyone who stands in our way. I'll even kill us both if it means we'll be together for eternity. That's how much I love you.'

I just sat there trembling. Something in the tone of his voice, in this disgusting house, surrounded by his sick writing on the wall, told me he was being deadly serious. I didn't know what to do or say, so I just sat there shaking until he made it clear he wanted yet more sex. I shook with fear during the whole horrible act. While he was panting away all I could feel was fear, shame and humiliation. My body went freezing cold, yet my palms were sweaty. I started to shudder.

He stopped mid-thrust and looked at me.

'Good,' he said. 'You're having an orgasm. I could tell you were loving it.'

No! No! I wanted to scream. This was not an orgasm. This was pure fear. I tried desperately to stop shaking but it was involuntary, like my body was communicating what I couldn't give voice to.

'What are you doing?' he shouted at me.

'Trying to stop shaking. I'm cold.'

'No, you're fucking not!' he screamed in my face. 'You're having an orgasm because I'm turning you on so much. Stop it!'

Even after it was over I continued to tremble. He seemed satisfied, but I was scared to say anything in case he started shouting again.

We got into the car in silence and he drove me home. I felt like I was being sucked into a vortex of pain and there was nothing I could do about it.

Chapter 8

I felt completely alone. Who could I talk to about my situation? There was no way I could tell my parents. That didn't even bear thinking about. I had no friends. I couldn't speak to my brother or sister, even though they had made their opinions clear about ST. Jason thought the man was a creep and Leanne just couldn't stand him. But despite their strong feelings, I felt I couldn't approach them. Although she was older, my sister didn't have that much experience with relationships either. It was not like we'd confided in each other about boys we liked growing up. We just never had those conversations, and the idea of suddenly landing this on her seemed weird to me. I continued to see a social worker, and would do so until I turned 18, but I didn't feel comfortable talking to her about this either. It felt like I was back to being that little girl in school – an alien, lost and afraid, with no one to turn to.

I was in this dark frame of mind when I went wandering through the town centre in Aberdare. I didn't have a purpose. I was just walking around, trying to make sense of life. A man approached me. He was trying to get people to sign up to a mobile-phone provider. He was of African descent, six foot tall and looked to be in his thirties. He was outgoing and friendly, as you'd have to be to work as a street salesman.

'Why so glum?' he said. He started with his patter, and although I made it clear I wasn't interested in what he was selling, he was so cheery that I couldn't help but smile.

'That's better,' he said, laughing. 'A smile doesn't cost anything.'

He started talking, not about mobile phones, but general things: what he thought of Aberdare, the weather. Before I knew what I was doing I was chatting to him, letting my guard down. It was like something inside me desperately needed someone – anyone – to talk to.

'Hey, I don't have to stand here all day doing this,' he said. 'Do you fancy getting a drink? We can chat some more.'

I shrugged. What the hell. He was nice. I liked talking to him. We went to the local Wetherspoon's pub. Once we were inside and had sat down, I don't know what came over me. I broke down. Obviously, the events of the last few weeks had got to me far more than I'd admitted to myself.

'It's okay,' he said gently. 'Let it out. You can talk to me. Talking is good.'

I didn't even know his name. I didn't ask him anything about himself. I was just so grateful to have someone to listen to me. And it all came out. I told him everything I was going through with ST. I told him I couldn't get out of this relationship, that ST was going to kill me or harm my father. I just sat there crying, telling him my life story.

He was sympathetic. He didn't seem to be judging me. He said it was terrible to hear all the things that I'd been through. He seemed like the opposite of ST. Maybe men weren't all like him. We sat there for a while talking before I said I'd better go home.

'No problem,' he said. 'I have some books I have to pick up from my flat, but how about we do that and then I'll take you home?'

I nodded. His flat wasn't far away. He shared it with five other people, all from different origins. The books were in his room and he told me to go with him while he got them. He sat me down on the bed and rummaged around under it, saying he was trying to find his books. When he jumped back up there were no books. I was just about to ask what was going on when he pushed me back and lay on top of me. I wanted to cry. What was it about me that made men think they could behave this way? No tears came, though. I'd used them all up earlier in the pub. Now I was just numb. Like ST, he didn't use a condom. When it was over I said I wanted to go home, but he kept me there for quite a while. I began to get really scared. I knew nothing about this man. I didn't even really know where he'd taken me, I'd been so caught up in the trauma of my tale. Finally, he said he would take me home.

When we got to my house ST was there waiting for me.

'Where have you been?' he said, actually sounding concerned. 'I was worried. You weren't answering your phone.'

The other man had disappeared, but ST could tell something had gone on. I was confused so I told him what had happened. I was so distressed that I almost didn't care about the consequences, even though I had no idea how he would react. To my astonishment, however, he was perfectly calm as he listened. When I had finished telling him he kissed me, made sure I was okay and left.

Although his reaction was a relief, I felt shocked to my core about what had happened. I kept replaying the events over and over in my head. After a couple of days I couldn't stand it anymore and told my mother. She was understandably shocked, horrified and desperately worried about me. She took me to see my GP, who advised me to take tests for HIV and other sexually transmitted diseases. Even though on some level I knew this man had raped me, I was in no fit state to go to the police or press charges. I didn't know who he was or even what his name was. I didn't see him again in the town centre.

When I next saw ST his attitude completely changed. Any compassion had gone.

'You led that guy on,' he said, when he brought it up. 'I bet you're having countless affairs, you slut.'

He demanded sex, as usual, but this time he was even more violent than usual, gripping my throat so tightly I thought my neck would snap, screaming, 'Slut!' into my face throughout. Afterwards he told me it was 'punishment sex' for what I'd done. He then made me lie down on the sofa and go over all the details of what had happened, from the colour of the man's bedroom walls and the toilet roll he used to how big his penis was. When I said, 'I don't know,' to any of his questions he shouted, 'Liar!' into my face.

It was almost like he enjoyed it. I had given him ammunition with which to punish me. As if he didn't have the upper hand before. It seemed that he had been digesting it in his mind, ready to bring it up at the right moment. I never mentioned to him that I had been tested for HIV. I never found out the results in any event. The clinic didn't notify me and I was too scared to ask.

In the days that followed I don't know how I carried on. The feeling of shame was so acute I struggled to breathe at times. I felt debased as a human being, like layers of my identity were being stripped away.

When he demanded I go and see him in his house, I didn't want to go but I felt I had no choice. As I left my home I could feel the tension building inside of me. I was due to catch a bus to Penrhiwceiber, but I needed to do something to relieve this pressure. I still had razor blades from when I self-harmed, so I sat down on the pavement, got a blade out of my handbag and started to cut myself right there in the street. I watched as blood seeped out of the wounds and trickled down my leg. The old feeling of satisfaction returned. This was something I could control amid the chaos. After I had finished I pulled my long white socks up. Within seconds they were soaked in blood, but I didn't care.

I got to his house and he saw right away the mess I was in. He knew, from what I had told him previously, about my self-harming. He didn't like it.

'I want to be the only one who hurts you,' he said.

I was in such a state of fear the words barely registered.

Not long after that he demanded I come over again. This time I said no. It was winter and the weather had closed in.

'Why can't you come?' he texted. I could sense the anger building.

'I've told you. We are completely snowed in.'

It was true. The snow was lying several inches thick. The roads were treacherous and public transport was struggling to run.

'Get here!'

The texts got more aggressive.

'I want to see you.'

'But I can't.'

'Now!'

'We are snowed in.'

'Walk! If you loved me you would do it. Are you saying you don't love me? You don't know what it would do to me if you said you didn't love me.'

'I do. But it's nearly eight miles.'

'Do it!'

It was now six months since this man had bulldozed his way into my life. The days when he had appeared happy-go-lucky, sympathetic and understanding were a distant memory. In its place was someone demanding, controlling and abusive.

I was seeing him all the time. And even on days like this, when the snow lay so thick on the ground it made travel impossible, he would not take no for an answer. I had no choice but to walk all the way to Penrhiwceiber, even though it would take several hours.

'You can't be serious,' my mum said, when she saw what I was going to do. 'This has gone too far.'

My parents had grown increasingly concerned for my welfare. I had not told them the full story of what went on with ST – how could I? But I didn't need to. They could tell from my demeanour and actions how utterly under his command I had become. And the incident with the mobile-phone man had made them realise how vulnerable I was.

'Sophie, you don't need to go,' my dad said. 'This is not healthy.'

They didn't understand. I had to go. I couldn't say no. Once he said something, I had to do it. If I didn't, he would get really nasty, and I knew how scary he could get – and how quickly.

'Sophie, please, this is madness.' My parents were pleading with me not to go as I stepped outside. It was so bitterly cold, and the slippery conditions underfoot meant it seemed to take forever. As I trudged through the snow I thought that at least he might be pleased I had done what I was told. And that was all I could hope for. It wasn't as though he would reward me for making the effort. There would be no loving embrace; no delight that I had walked all this way; no thoughtfully prepared dinner; no hot bath to warm me up after being out all this time in the freezing cold.

I knew what was in store for me. As soon as I got there

he would take me to the Green Room and violently have his way with me. Of that I could be certain. I knew now that the man who had appeared so friendly and non-threatening – so upbeat and charming – was in actual fact a depraved sex maniac. He demanded it all the time. And every time it was brutal. He launched his sexual assaults whenever he felt the urge – which was a lot.

I was under no illusions. I didn't try to convince myself that this was a loving relationship. There was no tenderness, no attempt to pleasure me or account for my feelings. It was all about his sexual gratification, which had to be serviced time and time again. There was nothing in it for me. He gave me nothing in return. Well, that's not strictly true. He had given me one thing during our time together – a sexually transmitted disease that my doctor confirmed was chlamydia when the pain down below had become unbearable. He'd given me that. And bruises. He had given me plenty of those. His attacks were so violent, so prolonged, that recently it had felt like my bruises had bruises.

The only thing I could be grateful for was that I hadn't fallen pregnant. It was a miracle I hadn't, as every time he demanded sex he refused to use protection. Perhaps it was a consequence of my eating disorders. Maybe it was my body's way of protecting itself. I don't know. All I knew was that I was terrified of it happening. It was the last thing I needed.

Why was I putting myself through this? It was simple. I was completely under his control. My mind was not my own. I left the house when he told me to. I stayed at his house for as long as he wanted me to. I ate when he ate. I washed when he wanted me to wash. When he wanted to sleep he expected me to sleep, but he continually complained that I was cold and made me sleep on the wooden floor. It was round-the-clock constant.

I lived for him. The only thing I had in my life was him. I had long since stopped going to the Socialist Party meetings. He had put an end to that. He wanted it to be him and me. He didn't want me speaking to anyone else.

By the time I made it to his house I couldn't feel my feet. My teeth were chattering. I was chilled to the bone.

'What took you so long?' he muttered, ushering me in without so much as a thanks for making such an effort. He led me to the Green Room, where he said he had something to show me on his computer. I was stunned as it registered what I was watching. A woman with blonde hair was being raped.

'That's disgusting,' I said, turning away.

'Watch it!' he yelled, yanking my arm so hard I thought he had broken it. He hauled me round and pushed me down on the airbed, pinning my arms so I couldn't move. 'Watch.'

I was no expert, but this was not normal hardcore pornography. It was sick, stomach-churning.

'Where did you find this? I said, shaking.

'The Dark Net,' he said, looking pleased with himself.

He had told me before about what a computer whizz he was and how he could access the underground Internet.

'Look,' he said, grabbing my head and forcing me to watch the woman scream in pain. 'That's you, isn't it?'

'What?' Was he insane? The woman had blonde hair but other than that she looked nothing like me.

'That's you.' His eyes darted between the screen and me. 'You're a whore. What are you doing starring in these films? I always knew you were a slut.'

I couldn't believe what I was hearing. Was he serious? Did he really think I would be involved in such a sick film? Or was he just saying it?

'It's not me.'

'Maybe you're right,' he said, studying it. 'You're a lot fatter than she is.'

That cut right to my heart. I might not have been in the grip of an eating disorder, but you never fully recover. Comments like that triggered my old insecurities.

'I'm not fat,' I said, trying to convince myself as much as him.

'Yes, you are.' He looked me up and down with an expression of disgust. 'When we first met you were nice and thin, but since then you've been putting on the beef.'

It wasn't the first time he had called me names. He regularly mocked me for taking antidepressants and medication for anxiety, calling me 'junky' or 'druggy', questioning why I would need them.

'I'm not fat,' I repeated.

'Let's see,' he said.

'What do you mean?'

'Take off your clothes?'

'What are you –'

'Take off your clothes! Now!' His face was pulsing red as he screamed.

I took off my clothes and stood naked before him.

'There!' he shouted, shoving me in front of a long mirror. I didn't want to look at the frightened little girl staring back.

'See what I mean?' he said, pulling at my stomach, thighs and anywhere else he fancied. 'Pudgy there, fat here, gross.'

He dragged me back in front of the computer. He brought up a porn site and scrolled through its images until he found the one he was after.

'See her?' I looked at a woman who must have been barely legal; she was so stick thin she looked ill. 'That's the type of body I want you to have.'

I was allowed to get dressed while he ordered pizza

from Domino's. When it arrived he took a slice and offered me the box. 'There you go,' he slobbered while chewing.

I shook my head.

'Well done!' He grinned, tomato sauce spilling from the corners of his mouth. 'That was a test.'

When he'd finished eating he returned to his disgusting video. He clearly got turned on watching such filth, as it was the prompter for him to take out his sexual frustration on me. He pinned me on the airbed like the woman in the video. As he acted out his sick fantasies I realised that this was where he was getting the inspiration for his violence. He was seeking out the most disturbing sexual films and trying to recreate them. It probably explained the penis stretcher, as the men in his video were much bigger.

I was just like the women in his videos – a rape victim. I'd never once consented to sex. He'd never asked my permission. I was just a sex toy to him, a ragdoll for him to use and abuse at will. It was all I could do to summon the strength to lie there and make it through. If he wasn't throwing me around, his hands were at my neck, choking me. One of these times he would go too far. I was sure of it.

When he'd finished and calmed down he went back to his computer. He showed me more films, this time of people getting cut up and mauled. There was blood and gore everywhere. I couldn't believe such material existed.

'I don't want to watch it, turn it off, turn it off,' I said. It was horrific. I felt tears welling up.

'Watch it!' he yelled in my face. 'You love it.'

He got his kicks from this as well. It was disgusting that something so abhorrent could turn him on, but it seemed to be that the more violent it was, the better. When his sexual urges were satisfied he turned to his other favourite subject – pestering me to move in with him.

'We have to be together,' he kept saying. 'I am the only person who can look after you. No one will ever love you like I do. I worship the ground you walk on.'

He was projecting extremely mixed messages – at times he seemed to hate being in my presence but then would flip to profess claims of undying love. I felt bewildered by it all.

'Not yet,' I said. The thought of moving into his place filled me with terror. It had become a house of horror. He might have control over me but this was something I had to resist.

'When?' he demanded.

'I don't know. It would be better to get a place together, not move in here.'

'I'll find us somewhere,' he said, making it sound more like a threat than a promise.

When I finally returned home my parents sat me down. My trudging through the snow to see this man had been the final straw for them.

'You have to stop seeing him,' they said. I could see the desperation in their eyes. They only wanted the best for me, as always, but they just didn't understand my situation. How could I tell them I was under the control of a sex maniac?

I couldn't begin to tell them what I was going through. It was so utterly shameful. Some of the things he did to me I wanted to erase from my memory banks, like when he slapped me across the face with his erect penis before ejaculating on my face. It was disgusting. It made me feel like an idiot, sickened and totally out of my depth. I was convinced I was guilty of something, especially when he had grabbed me by the jacket in Aberdare Park, when I had tried to walk away from him, and he had repeated his threat to tell my father what I was 'really like'.

Some hardcore sexual things he forced me to do made me feel like I had committed a crime. I couldn't tell anyone these things, least of all my parents.

'What are these?' they said, pointing to my wrists. I hadn't realised the bruises were visible. 'Was this him? Is he hurting you?'

I pulled my top down to cover them up. 'It's nothing,' I said. 'I bruise easily, that's all.'

'Sophie, this man is dangerous. You have to stop seeing him.'

'I can't stop seeing him,' I said. Trying to sound defiant, I added, 'And you can't tell me what to do.'

They took matters into their own hands. They spoke to my social worker and told her that if it came to it, they would lock me in my room to stop me seeing this man. They were stunned with the response they got. The social worker said, 'Oh, if you do that she can press charges against you.'

'Don't you understand?' my dad said. 'What are we supposed to do? She is going with an older man. He is hurting her. She is a vulnerable person with a history of health issues. She's in danger.'

The social worker said there was nothing she could do unless I did or said something against him. I did once mention to her that he could get quite violent at times, and I showed her bruises on my wrists, but she acted like she wasn't interested.

My parents spoke to my mental-health team but were met with the same attitude. They still didn't give up. They spoke to the police about the possibility of putting a restraining order on him to prevent him coming anywhere near me, on the grounds that I was vulnerable and not capable of knowing whether I was in danger. They explained that I was socially inexperienced and hadn't been out of the house for all the years of my childhood. I had these conditions, they said, and he was a much older man, but the police officers they spoke to just shrugged and said their hands were tied unless I made a complaint. It was tough for my parents to hear.

It seemed like nobody cared. No one wanted to know. My parents were helpless, and the situation started to put an enormous strain on my dad's health. He was very poorly as it was, and now his condition deteriorated further. He hated me seeing ST. He begged me to stop.

He didn't realise that I had to see him. It felt like a matter of life or death. That was what it came down to. I was scared to end things in case ST did something to hurt my dad. What I didn't realise was that by continuing to see him I was doing precisely that.

It came to a head one day when I was at home. I had hardly been there for days and they were worried sick. I was in my room when I heard a commotion. An emergency doctor arrived. I didn't know what was going on.

'He's having a heart attack,' my mum said, her eyes full of tears.

They rushed him to hospital.

Oh God, no, I thought. *Please make him be okay.*

I waited nervously at home, praying for good news. It came later that day. Dad had survived a heart attack, but it had been touch and go. He might have died if it hadn't been for the fast response of the medics.

I was consumed with guilt. I had brought this on. I

hadn't meant to. I had been trying to protect him. ST demanded to know where I was and why I wasn't seeing him. I called him to tell him the news. I could hardly get the words out I was crying so much.

'It's okay,' he said. 'You have me. That's all you need.'

I wanted to see Dad in hospital.

'You're not going on your own,' ST said. 'I will come with you.'

As soon as we got there I knew it was a mistake. He was a disgrace, mucking around, putting latex gloves on and making rude jokes to nurses and my family. He skipped around the wards and made a big show of kissing me in front of people. One of the nurses came up to me and said she would tell him to leave if his behaviour continued. It was a complete embarrassment. I never visited my dad again in hospital.

My dad was effectively out of the picture, unable to stand up to me anymore. My mum and sister never said anything to me, but I was sure they blamed me for Dad's heart attack. They were colder towards me. I had always been so close to Mum, but I felt us drifting apart. Who could blame her? She had tried everything. Plus, she was taken up with worry for my father. They didn't need to tell me how they felt. I knew it myself. I had a gnawing feeling inside me that this was all my fault. I blamed myself but never told anyone. My brother tried his best to help me.

When ST called and said, 'I want you down here right now,' and I immediately replied, 'Okay, I'll get a taxi,' Jason stopped me at the door.

'Please don't go, Soph,' he said. It was heartbreaking to watch. He was crying.

'I have to go,' I said.

'You don't. You can stay. I'll protect you.' He was on the floor, grabbing me by the leg.

'I have to go. You don't understand.' I pushed him aside and ran into the waiting taxi.

They just didn't get it. If he said, 'Jump,' I said, 'How high?' I was under his total control. He was closing in all the time. He was all I thought about. I had put my life on hold for him. His claws were well and truly into me. He had got what he wanted. He had turned me against my family. Before I met him I'd never argued with my family, yet now we seemed to be regularly at each others' throats. He was always there, fuelling the fire and taking me further and further away from them.

In that moment I effectively turned my back on my family. They had tried everything in their power to save me from the evil that had invaded our home, but it wasn't enough. I made my decision. The consequences would be mine to deal with.

The taxi delivered me to the house of horror. I got out and ran into his arms. He held me, for once playing the part of the caring boyfriend.

'I am all you need, Sophie,' he said, stroking my hair. 'I'm the one who is going to look after you now. You don't have to worry. I am the only one you need. I will always be there to protect you. Always. It will just be me and you – forever.'

That was what terrified me.

Chapter 9

We were walking back to his house from the shops. As always he gripped my hand and pulled me in close, like I was an errant dog on a tight leash. Then his grip loosened and he almost pushed me away. A woman approached. I didn't recognise her.

'Hey, there,' she said to him, like he was an old friend. She looked much older than me, with greasy blonde hair scraped back from her face. His face lit up – something I hadn't seen since the early days, when he'd pursued me. He obviously knew her.

'Who's this?' the woman said, glancing in my direction.

'Just a friend,' he said, moving so he was in between us, almost blocking her from seeing me. I stood there feeling awkward. She played with her ponytail as they exchanged words. They were clearly flirting. Was she an ex-girlfriend? Someone he wanted to be his girlfriend?

After a brief chat she walked off and we carried on down the street.

'So who was she?' I asked, once we were back inside the house.

'None of your fucking business,' he yelled, pushing me so hard I fell against the wall, banging my head. I yelped in pain and he grabbed me, hauled me to my feet and marched me to the Green Room, where I kept a bag with my few belongings.

'Get out, you fucking whore!' he screamed in my face. I couldn't understand why he was going so crazy. He dragged me to the corner where my things were. 'Take your things and get out.'

I hurriedly tried to pack the clothes I had into the bag, but he grabbed it off me before I had a chance to close it. He gripped my arm tightly, wrenched the bag from my grasp and marched me, my feet dragging on the wooden floor, to the front door. He swung the door open so violently I thought it might come off its hinges. Without another word he threw my bag into the street, my clothes streaming out onto the road. Then, with two hands, he shoved me after it and I stumbled across the pavement. I heard the door slam shut, the noise echoing down the street. Curtains twitched in the houses opposite as I got to my feet, picked up my clothes and stuffed them back into my bag.

What the hell was all that about? I didn't know what

to do, so I walked aimlessly back towards the town centre. I hadn't got very far when my phone rang. It was him. He seemed to have calmed down.

'I'm sorry,' he said. 'Come back. But that was your fault. You made me do that.'

What? Was he serious?

'Anyway, get back here now.'

I didn't know what to think. How could it have been my fault? Was it because I was there? Was he angry because we'd bumped into someone else he had been seeing? I'd had my suspicions, particularly after contracting the sexually transmitted disease. Was I stupid to think I was the only one he had been having sex with?

When I got back to the house I saw he had written more things on the wall – sexual rantings, words like 'bitch', and there were things about 'the end of the world' I hadn't seen before – all scrawled in red, black and blue marker pen.

'You don't know what you do to me, Sophie. This is the effect you have on me.'

He launched into a tirade about how much he loved me. All I kept thinking about were the things he wasn't telling me.

I realised that there were lots of things I didn't know. Not long after this incident, we were walking in the park. He was very particular about the route we took. We'd walked for a bit when a large-built woman, with short grey hair and glasses, approached with a little boy, who looked far too young to be her son. As we got closer I saw that he recognised her.

'Hello. What a surprise,' he said, before turning to me. 'This is my mum.'

It certainly was a surprise – that they'd just happened to bump into each other. Had they arranged this between themselves before we left the house?

The little boy was shaking and, despite attempts by ST and his mum, was not for talking.

'He's very shy,' ST's mum said.

'He's my little cousin, Luke,' ST said, rubbing his hair.

The more he tried to engage with Luke the more nervous the boy looked. In fact, as I studied him I could have sworn he had a look on his face that I recognised – one of fear.

ST's mum suggested we sit on a park bench. She lifted the boy up onto ST's knee and got out her phone to take a photo. Now the boy looked very scared and was shaking uncontrollably.

'He must be cold,' ST's mum said, even though Luke was perfectly wrapped up for the weather. She took the photo and, after a short exchange, we went on our way.

Seeing his mum prompted me to ask him questions about his own family, which he rarely talked about. He shut down conversations along those lines, and he did so this time too. It occurred to me that I didn't really know much about this man. Even things like why he lived in care when his parents were still alive were a mystery to me. When I asked about that part of his life he just made out that it was a time when he was young and stupid. He seemed to suggest his reckless days were behind him. If only that were true.

Never was he more reckless than when he was behind the wheel of his dilapidated motor. I hated getting in the car with him. I was a nervous car passenger anyway, after what had happened with my dad. There were too many factors that could go wrong. And with him behind the wheel anything could happen. He loved to speed and thought the rules of the road didn't apply to him. I felt especially nervous when he was in such a volatile mood, which he was on the day he suggested we go for a drive in the country. I started to feel anxious. It didn't help that it had been raining, which I knew would make the roads even more slippery than normal.

He was in one of those moods that told me it was best not to argue. I reluctantly got in and reached for the seatbelt.

'Leave it,' he shouted. 'What do you need that for? You're with me.'

Even though his car felt like it was falling apart, he took off as though it was a sports car. I gripped the door handle so tightly my knuckles were white, and gasped as he took a roundabout the wrong way, the blare of car horns ringing in my ears.

My heart was in my mouth. I didn't want to look as he shouted obscenities at other motorists and turned the stereo up. He was heading up the mountains to Llanwonno, a little village high up in the mountains, about twenty minutes from Aberdare. The road had lots of twisty bends. Several times I thought we'd crash, but the other drivers managed to take evasive action. Somehow we made it up the hill in one piece. On a clear day it is a pretty spot, with views over the Rhondda and Cynon valleys. This was not one of those days. I could barely take in my surroundings. The dank autumn afternoon, the sky grey and heavy with an air of impending doom, mirrored my own mood.

'Can we just go back, please?' I said, not long after we'd stopped.

He barely spoke but didn't seem happy at the suggestion. When he took off again it was even faster than usual.

'Slow down!' I said, as he careered around a couple of tight bends, my grip on the handle tightening.

'Stop being pathetic,' he roared, taking delight in scaring me.

He had to swerve to avoid a car when he took a bend too wide. I gasped. That was close. He stopped laughing, but only for a moment before he hammered the accelerator once more.

'You're going to kill us,' I screamed.

'At least we'll die together, then.'

The car creaked as we sped on down the mountain. There were no airbags in this rust bucket. I imagined the brake pads were non-existent. There was another near miss as the car's back end slipped on another bend.

'That was close,' he laughed. 'SHIT!'

We hit a patch of wet leaves. He yanked the wheel but it made no difference. The road curved; we went straight: off the tarmac, over the verge and down a slope. The car rolled, there was a great crash and groaning of metal. I was thrown forwards, sideways and back; forwards, sideways and back.

It seemed like we rolled forever, but finally we came to rest. The windscreen and passenger window were shattered. My whole left side and back burned with a searing pain. I was scared to look at first, but when I summoned the courage I saw that my left arm was ripped to pieces and bone looked like it was sticking out of the skin at my elbow. Blood soaked my clothes.

Before I could really take stock of what had happened, he had jumped out of the car and was at my side. There didn't appear to be a mark on him.

'Wait,' I said, but he was already dragging me out of the car. I flopped onto the wet grass, in even more pain than before. 'What happened?'

'We hit a patch of wet leaves, I think,' he said.

I slumped back on the earth, aware of him chattering away on the phone. I lay shaking and bleeding, trying to determine what was broken, for what seemed like an eternity before the medics arrived. They fitted me with a neck brace and strapped me to a stretcher, telling me it was a precaution in case of spinal injuries. The strict restraints made me feel claustrophobic and I started to panic, fearful that his dragging me from the wreckage might have left me crippled.

They carried me to the roadside and the waiting ambulance. After we arrived at hospital and they examined my injuries, a consultant explained that I was lucky. I had no spinal problems and, despite severe cuts, no bones were broken. I would need an operation on my arm and back to remove glass, however.

He, on the other hand, had survived without a scratch.

Despite my requests, he refused to call my mum to tell her what had happened. She had to ring the hospital daily for updates. He wouldn't leave my side and blocked my family's attempts to see me. One of the doctors eventually told him to ring Mum to keep her updated. My dad was still recovering from his heart attack, so this was the last thing my mother needed. Not knowing the full extent of my injuries only made matters worse.

He seemed more concerned about the car, which was a write-off.

After three weeks in hospital the doctors said I was well enough to go home, wherever that was. Despite nearly killing me, ST used the car crash as proof we should live together permanently.

'I was the one who was there for you,' he said, 'not your family.'

I wanted to see my family, though, and this sent him into a foul mood. He made cruel comments about them and made me feel guilty for leaving him, even though it was only going to be for a few hours. When I did finally see my parents it was clear that they had hoped the crash would be a watershed moment. Surely after something like that I would cut him out of my life? They were not prepared, then, when I told them, 'He wants me to move in with him permanently.'

They were horrified. Apart from having a few clothes and belongings at his house, I suppose my home was still at Mum and Dad's. They knew if I moved out completely that would be it. They would never see me.

'Is that really what you want to do?' Mum asked.

I shook my head. I couldn't tell them what his place was like, with its large, cold, dilapidated rooms that he had never cleaned or tried to make in any way presentable in all the time he had lived there. He hadn't added to the furniture, so his laptop and microwave still sat on the floor along with his clothes and shoes, which were piled in corners of the room. To tell my parents I tolerated that mess would be admitting that my standards had plummeted from those they had instilled in me.

'I don't want to move in to the place he has,' I told them. For a moment they looked relieved. That's until I added: 'I've said it would be better if we got a place together.'

The looks on their faces said it all. It was the stuff of nightmares for two loving parents. They knew their daughter was making a huge mistake, but there was nothing they could do about it.

He had warmed to the suggestion of us getting a place together. He wanted to move to Brecon, twenty-five miles away. That thought terrified me. I wanted to be close to home.

'Why don't we move to somewhere around here for a while and then maybe move to Brecon,' I said. He didn't look convinced. I decided that if I was to have some sort of control, I'd have to take on the job of house hunting. If I left it to him he'd drag me off to another rundown hellhole.

I found a little semi-detached cottage for rent two streets away from my parents' house in Trecynon. We went to look at it. The front door led to the kitchen, with a bathroom opposite. From the kitchen was the living room, and then up the stairs there was a little landing, which led to a small dressing room and the property's one bedroom. It was on the market unfurnished, but I thought I could make it look nice. I had been receiving benefits in the form of disability living allowance because I was considered not fit to work, so I had some money to spend on it. Plus, once I turned 18 in a few weeks' time, I would have access to my compensation from my dad's car accident, which was being held in a trust fund.

ST liked it and agreed to take it. Thank God. My situation was by no means ideal, but at least I was exerting a small bit of control, and I was relieved my parents would be close at hand.

When the time came to sign the contracts, we met with the landlord. Looking at the piece of paper suddenly brought home what I was doing. Up to that moment it seemed like I had been sleepwalking. He had engineered everything and manipulated me to do what he said. This was different. I was pushing this – so he wouldn't whisk me off miles away from anyone. I might have been under his control, but I wanted to be close to my parents. The thought of being stuck with him in the middle of nowhere terrified me. In a remote cottage he could kill me and it would take weeks for anyone to notice.

The landlord handed me the pen and showed me where to sign. My hand was shaking. I really didn't want to sign it.

'Take a moment,' the landlord said, and showed me outside. 'Listen, love,' he said, once we were out of earshot. 'Do you really want to do this?'

This was it. I could back out. There was still time. How could I, though? If I didn't go through with this, he could kill me or hurt my family.

'I'm fine,' I said, composing myself. 'Yes, I'll sign it.'

We went back inside. I took the pen and signed my life away.

Chapter 10

He was delighted with the house. 'We'll name it Magnetic Cottage,' he said, 'as we are both sides of the magnet. I am north and you are south.'

By the time we moved in a short while after, I was determined to try to make the best of it. I used my money to buy a green leather sofa. I put butterfly stickers over the walls and added rose garlands across the curtain rails and going up the stairs. I selected a piece of really nice wall art for the top of the stairs. The bedroom was small. There was only space for the horrible airbed in there, but I painted it red and white to provide a splash of colour. I hung two large mirrors on the wall. In the kitchen I put up an Etch A Sketch toy to make drawings on.

My intention was to make it look like a proper home, the type normal couples might have. I should have known better. Although he liked the house and was enthusiastic about moving in, his idea of appropriate was in another dimension to mine.

He had become obsessed with taking photos of me, and he insisted on putting them everywhere. I tried to limit him to one or two but he demanded more. The house became like a shrine to me. It was intensely creepy. But it was nothing compared to what he next put up on the wall – a times-tables chart.

'Why are you putting that up?' I asked.

'So you can recite them.'

'I don't need a chart. I know my times tables.'

He leered at me. 'You left school so early it's up to me to teach you now. You're going to recite them to me so I know how much you've learned.'

He seemed fixated on the fact that I'd left school early. Even though I was highly academic, in his eyes I was still a primary-school child.

'This is ridiculous,' I said. 'I've told you what having Asperger's means.'

'Oh, yes, you have Asperger's, whatever that means,' he said mockingly. 'It's just a made-up condition that really means you're just a dumbass. I want to see you revise your times tables and then I'll test you.'

He was deadly serious. I rattled through the tables.

'Not like that,' he said, shaking his head. 'Stop showing off. Get some wrong.'

Now I was confused. Either he thought I was stupid or this was just a game. I quickly realised I had to play along. He pulled me onto his lap and asked me to recite them again. This time I deliberately got some wrong. He corrected me, and when he asked them again and I got them right, he said, 'Clever girl. You're learning.'

When it came to meal times the creepiness continued. He made macaroni cheese but only gave me little bits to eat.

'I want to feed you,' he said, and I had to sit there, like a toddler in a high chair, while he got the fork and fed me. When he'd finished I was still hungry.

'Can I have some more?'

'No,' he said, finishing the last of it. 'We don't want you to get fat now, do we? If you eat that, it will go straight to your ass.'

Any comment about my weight or size really upset me. I tried not to let him show how much, though. Since meeting him I'd lost loads of weight and was starting to get really thin again. He liked me this way.

'Your ideal weight is four stone,' he said.

I couldn't believe what I was hearing. That was two stone less than I was when the doctor threatened to hospitalise me.

'That wouldn't be healthy,' I said. 'I've been there before and it's not pleasant, believe me.'

'I'd like to see it, though.' He was getting his kicks from this, as if he loved the idea of me being tiny and skinny, like a little girl. He pinched my arms and legs. 'You could still do with losing some of this fat.'

'The reason I take my medication is because I had an eating disorder. You know that.'

'I know you're a junky,' he said. 'Popping those pills to make you happy. It's stupid. You're with me now. Stop taking them.'

'You can't just come off drugs like this,' I said. 'It would be dangerous.'

'I'm your carer now,' he said menacingly. 'I'll decide what's best for you.' His hand moved to my neck and he squeezed tightly. I couldn't breathe. 'Got that?'

I tried to protest, but he got up and found my packets of antidepressants and diazepam.

'What are you doing?' I was scared. I needed my pills.

'Showing you it's a waste of time taking them.'

He ran to the bathroom, tipped them down the pan and flushed them away.

'No!' I cried, trying to stop him, but he held me off with one hand, laughing. I tried to wrestle free but he pushed me hard. I stumbled backwards and fell to the floor. He picked me up and put me over his shoulder.

'I think you need teaching a lesson,' he said, carrying me upstairs.

He threw me on the bed and tore my top off, ripping it at the neck. I screamed but he pinned me down, got the rest of my clothes off and was on top of me, growling in my ear like a crazed beast. As he thrust himself into me he pushed my neck down so hard I was sure he would break it.

'I want to make you bleed down there,' he growled.

There were no limits to his depravity. When he was finally finished, he pawed at my hair and demanded I admit to him that I had been sexually abused as a child. It was like he desperately wanted it to be true. I was in tears, asking him to stop. He just laughed.

That night, as I lay shaking in the dark – the realisation dawning that, for all my attempts at homemaking, this was going to be yet another house of horrors – my head started throbbing. As the night wore on it got worse. I thought at first it might be the lack of food, but then it struck me. I had missed my last dose of medication before he destroyed the rest. This was part of the withdrawal symptoms. The doctor had warned me that if I came off the medication suddenly it could be catastrophic. Any reduction in dosage had to be managed carefully to give the body time to adapt. I risked having a stroke or heart attack. The medication had been my lifeline. It had given me the confidence to leave the house. How would I cope without it?

In the morning I felt sick and the sweat was pouring off me – like a junky going cold turkey.

'I said you were a junky,' he mocked, when I told him how terrible I felt. 'Get over it. There is nothing wrong with you.'

'You don't understand,' I pleaded. 'I can feel my anxiety returning.'

He shook his head. 'Don't be stupid. I'll protect you. You are with me now. It is me and you. I am the only one taking care of you now. You don't need doctors and shrinks.'

I had a new crutch now. I was under his spell and too ill to appreciate the full implications of what he was saying. It became clear over the next few days. He demanded power of attorney over my finances. He made me sign over my benefits into his name. He demanded control over the compensation money when it came. I was too weak to argue. For days my whole body shook, my head felt like it would burst and it was like I was wasting away. I just wanted it to stop.

He cut up all my bank cards in front of me. 'I'm all you need now,' he said.

On the wall he pinned up a list of vows.

'We're as good as married now, me and you,' he said, when I looked at it. 'So these are the vows you will promise to live by.'

It was things like 'I promise to honour and obey, till death do us part, in sickness and in health, for better or worse, richer or poorer'.

'Do you promise?'

I nodded, too weak to resist.

'And because we're now married we should start a family. It's time we got you pregnant and had a baby … to make our lives complete.'

Now he had my attention. There was no way I could contemplate bringing a baby into this nightmare. It was unthinkable. This man should not be in the same room as a child, let alone be a dad. It was still a miracle I had not fallen pregnant, given the amount of times I'd had unprotected intercourse. I couldn't afford not to take precautions.

Slowly, I got over the withdrawal symptoms from coming off my medication. It wasn't easy but I knew I had to get stronger to look after myself. There was no point trying to get another prescription, as he would only find the tablets and the consequences didn't bear thinking about.

I did see my GP, though – to go on the pill. I didn't want to leave anything to chance. Being on the pill at least gave me some reassurance that the nightmare scenario wouldn't materialise – for now, anyway.

I had been taking the pill for a few weeks when, one morning, I looked for the packet where I'd hidden it, above a cupboard in the kitchen, and my heart stopped. It wasn't there. I looked everywhere, thinking I might have put it somewhere else and forgotten. I hadn't. There was no way I could ask him where it was. But I had my suspicions. He must have found it and got rid of it.

'I want you to give me a baby, Sophie,' he said repeatedly.

Without contraception, how could I stop that horror from happening?

'Why don't we get a puppy first and then think about having a baby?' I said to him. I could tell he wasn't thrilled about the idea of letting a dog into the cottage, but he relented.

I immediately set about finding one. I had my heart set on a Cavalier King Charles spaniel and found a breeder in Tenby. As soon as I saw the dogs I fell in love. They were tiny bundles of white and brown fur with eyes like deep pools of melted chocolate. One in particular seemed to take a shine to me. She was the answer to my prayers and I named her Star. Finally, I felt I had my first true friend in the world.

As anyone who has reared a puppy knows, they demand a lot of attention. It takes a lot of work to get them house-trained. I fussed over her, cuddled her, and in just a few days we formed a close bond.

Although he had agreed that I could get one, he didn't want anything to do with her at first, which suited me fine. It meant our bond grew stronger. As my focus went on Star he became increasingly jealous. He made cruel comments about her, saying what a pathetic creature she was because she couldn't fend for herself. He grabbed her roughly and said how easily it would be for him to kill her.

'Just one snap of the neck,' he said, laughing.

That made me want to cuddle her more and make an even greater fuss. I knew he was violent with me, but surely he wouldn't want to hurt a defenceless animal.

Not long after we got her I had to go out for a doctor's appointment. I would only be away for an hour.

'Don't go,' he said. 'Don't leave me.'

'It's only one hour.'

'It might seem like only one hour, but if you left me for one hour every week, by the time you were 60 that would mean we would have spent 2,184 hours apart,' he said, with complete seriousness. 'We need to be together all the time.'

I didn't know what to say, but I left anyway. When I came back I could sense something had happened. I opened the front door and, even though it was still light outside, the house was in darkness. It took me a moment to work out why. He had put black curtains over the windows. I put a light on and caught my breath. On the Etch A Sketch in the kitchen was written 'BITCH!' That wasn't all. It looked like dirt had been smeared on the wall. It only took a moment to register that it was dog faeces. Oh God, where was Star?

I found them in the living room. He was sitting in the darkness, holding Star by the scruff of her neck. She looked terrified.

'What have you done?'

He let her go and she jumped down and came towards me, but I could see she was limping.

'It's that animal,' he said. 'It's disgusting, pooing everywhere.'

'What have you done to her?' I cuddled her close to me. Her heart was pounding but she licked my face, obviously so relieved to see me.

'I had to tell her off for making such a mess.'

From then on he used her as a tool against me. When I said I wanted to pop round to see my mum, which was just around the corner, he threatened to hurt Star if I left her behind. When I said I'd take her with me, he grabbed her by the neck. 'If you go, it's the last time you'll see her alive.' I had no choice but to stay.

Seeing the effect it had on me, he threatened her with violence to get me to do anything he wanted. He put on a disturbing film, and when I said I didn't want to watch it he picked up Star and threatened to throw her against the wall.

I prayed that it was a phase and he would calm down and come round to the idea of having her in the house, but his attitude only hardened towards her.

He started smoking a lot of cannabis, which I thought was meant to make people mellow and peace-loving. It seemed to make him even more volatile. As Christmas approached I tried to make the house look festive with a tree and some decorations. He was getting off his head on dope. When I'd finished decorating the house I asked him what he thought.

'Not bad,' he said, 'but you're missing something.'

'What?' I said, looking round, puzzled.

He grabbed Star, who had been sleeping in her basket. 'A Star for the top of the tree!'

'Don't!' I yelled, but before I could stop him he'd lifted her up and rammed her into the top of the tree. She tried to find something to grip onto but fell through the branches to the floor amid a cascade of baubles and tinsel. I ran to her and cuddled her in my arms. She was whimpering and trembling.

'You love that bloody animal more than me,' he shouted.

I shielded her from him. He was right, of course. I did love her more than him, but I couldn't admit it. I had no idea what he was capable of.

'Give it to me,' he growled. 'It's going on the bloody tree.'

I held her into me but he was too strong. He ripped

her by her neck from my grasp. I watched helplessly as he spun and threw her against the wall. There was a sickening crack with the impact and she fell to the floor in a heap.

I froze, not knowing what to do. She somehow got to her feet, a little unsteady. She seemed dazed but was able to walk. I didn't know how she hadn't broken every bone in her body.

I ran out through the kitchen and she followed me. He grabbed her again and tossed her back inside. It was emptying down with rain. I stood outside and watched her try again to reach me. This time he picked her up and threw her onto the patio beside me.

'If you fucking love her so much you can join her,' he said. 'That thing is not getting back into the house.'

He slammed the door. I heard the key turn as I gathered her into me. She was soaked through, crying, her whole body shaking. I was shivering too but I hoped she'd get some warmth from me. I debated over what to do. My parents were just around the corner. They loved animals, but if I turned up like this I'd have to tell them what had happened. I had no choice but to stand there in the freezing rain and hope he'd see sense and let us back in.

After a few minutes it became clear that he was trying to punish me. I knocked on the door. When that didn't get a response I went round and knocked on the window.

I couldn't see in because of the black curtains. No doubt he was in there smoking more cannabis and watching sick videos. My hands were numb. I didn't have a jacket. It was December, the light was going and I was frozen to my bones.

Eventually, after nearly two hours, he opened the door and let us in.

'I want that thing gone,' he said.

After that I knew I couldn't keep Star. Her life was in danger as long as she remained in that house. It broke my heart but I asked around to see if anyone would take her. My mum and dad still had their two spaniels, Angel and Sammy, but they weren't friendly to other dogs, so that wasn't an option. I asked my aunt and grandmother to take her, but they wouldn't. My gran said, 'Tell him to leave and keep the dog.' If only it were that simple.

I posted an advert on a pet website – but I wasn't moving fast enough.

'I thought you were getting rid of that stupid mutt,' he said.

Star tried to keep out of his way but he'd seek her out, aim kicks at her and constantly harass her. He was in a permanent bad mood and took everything out on the dog.

'I'm trying to find a home for her,' I said.

'If you can't find one, I'll sort it.' With that he ran to her, picked her up and threw her out onto the patio.

He slammed the door. I knew that if I went after her he'd attack me or, worse, take it out on her. After a moment he went out, slamming the door behind him. I waited a while before going out to check Star was okay. I wasn't sure if this was a trap to see how quickly I ran to her.

I opened the door to let her in and my heart stopped. There was blood smeared down the wall opposite. I had to put a hand out to stop myself collapsing. Oh my God. My Star. My poor defenceless little puppy. What had he done to her? I started crying. Then I heard scuffling from behind the bin. I looked up and saw her little face peeking round. She was okay! She ran towards me. I couldn't believe it. After fearing the worst, I was so relieved she was alive and unhurt.

How had he been able to smear blood on the wall, though? I shuddered at the possibilities. Had he got hold of someone else's pet around here? God knows what he had done to get that much blood.

When a woman contacted me later that day about the advert online I told her to come straight away. There was no time to vet her and check her suitability. If he came home to find Star still there, he would kill her.

The woman seemed nice enough and fell instantly for Star.

'I can give her to you now,' I said. 'But only on the condition that you keep me updated on her development. I want to see photographs occasionally so I know she's okay.'

The woman nodded. 'Of course. She's going to a good home. Don't you worry.'

I gave Star a last kiss and cuddle, silently thanking her for the love and joy she had given me in the few short weeks we had known each other, and praying that she wouldn't suffer any more once she was away from this monster.

When the woman left I burst into tears. I'd never known emotional pain like it. My heart was breaking.

Her new owner never did get in touch. I have no idea how my little Star has been without me.

He was delighted when he came home and I told him she'd gone.

'I've finally got you back to myself,' he kept saying, over and over. 'Nothing will come between us again.'

I was bereft. It felt like my one companion in the world had gone. Now I was most definitely on my own.

Chapter 11

Turning 18 is supposed to be a magical time – the moment a child becomes an adult, a milestone birthday when so much changes. I was able to vote, get married without the consent of my parents, be in control of my own medical treatment.

Why, then, did it feel like I had less freedom than when I was a child, locked inside a world of anxiety and shut away from a society that scared me so much? It had taken me years to overcome the limitations imposed upon me by my condition – only to immediately lose the independence I'd fought so hard to win for myself. Eighteen might be a landmark birthday for some – but not me. I awoke to find no cards, no presents, no balloons, no oversized keys and no one wishing me 'Happy Birthday'.

The only comment that confirmed he knew the significance of the day was: 'So when do you get your money?' He did nothing to acknowledge the moment. The only thing he gave me was a couple of hours to go and spend with my family. It was always nice to see my parents but being home brought a different kind of stress. My dad was still very ill, and seeing him struggle and the strain my mother was under only made me feel more guilt at my part in their troubles. They did their best to mark my birthday, but when they asked me how I was I lied and said everything was fine. How could I begin to tell them?

My birthday meant I finally had access to my trust fund. He had been itching to get his hands on my compensation ever since our car accident. Being without wheels had been driving him even madder than normal, and I suspected that he had been counting the days until he got access to my windfall. The compensation was a significant amount of money, and over the years had grown into a pot of several-thousand pounds. Not that I saw any of it.

As soon as he got his hands on my trust fund he treated himself to a new PlayStation, a projector screen for his sick videos and some computer equipment. But the item he was most keen on was a motorbike. I thought it might be the death of him. He took off on it at such a speed and refused to wear a helmet. He seemed to think he was invincible and immune from the police. Given the way he drove a car, you could see why. With the bike, however, it was a different story. He had only been out on it a few times when the police pulled him over, discovered that, among other things, he had no insurance and charged him with various offences. He went to court and received a suspended sentence with the condition that he had to wear a tag so he couldn't leave the house after a certain time.

The police also came to confiscate his beloved bike. He was furious. We were outside in the lane when a neighbour's cat approached, just being friendly. Without warning, he booted the animal so hard with his biker boots the cat went flying. Luckily, it managed to run away, but I couldn't hide my disgust.

'Oh my God, that's so cruel,' I shouted, getting flashbacks of how he was with Star. This was the man who had first charmed me with talk of his love of animals.

He grabbed me by the throat. 'You don't know the meaning of cruel,' he hissed. 'They're dumb, stupid animals. I've strangled a cat with my bare hands before.'

He released his grip and I gasped for breath. Given how he had treated Star, I believed him. What sort of psycho hurts poor, defenceless animals?

'It's not right to hurt animals,' I said.

'Shut the fuck up,' he said, pushing me inside. I didn't say another word after that.

He was not supposed to drive but he ignored that – and his curfew. He went out and bought another motorbike almost immediately. It was a black Suzuki racing motorbike that he boasted could do 150 mph. This time he had bought a helmet – but to my horror he then produced a pink one for me.

What I would have loved to say was: 'There's no way I'm getting on that thing with you, as the last time you nearly killed us both.' But I knew that if I did he would probably have grabbed me by the neck. All I said instead was: 'Are you sure this is a good idea?'

'Of course! You'll ride pillion.'

Nerves jangling, I climbed onto the bike. He grabbed my hands and showed me where to grip. He took off so fast that I thought I'd fly off the back. I held on for dear life. He screamed as the bike went faster and faster, but I couldn't make out a word over the roar of the engine and the wind. I shut my eyes and prayed for it to end.

The next time he wanted me to come out with him was for a night ride to Swansea. Given that he was on a curfew and had a suspended sentence for good behaviour, it was risky. I felt sick, perhaps at the thought of being on that bike with him for such a long drive. For once, he didn't force me to go with him.

I expected him to be out for most of the night, but when he hadn't returned by the morning I wondered if something had happened to him. Come nightfall he still wasn't back. I thought I'd better investigate in case he had suffered a crash. I found a number for his mum and called her. She was immediately convinced something terrible had happened. She said she would ring round the hospitals to see if he'd been admitted to A&E and she would report him missing to the police.

Another day passed and still we had no idea what had happened to him. There was no record of a motorbike accident and no one fitting his name or description had been admitted to hospital.

While I was waiting for news, a relative of his named James called round to the cottage. All I knew about him was that he was someone ST liked to get stoned with.

'Have you heard anything?' James said. He wasn't as tall as ST but he still towered over me. I told him I didn't have any news. He invited himself in and was lingering about. I started to feel uneasy.

'So he's just left you here all alone?' he said, hovering around in the kitchen. I moved towards the door so I could show him out. 'He's told me a lot about you.' Now I definitely wanted him to leave. He moved towards me. 'As he's not here, you know, you and I could –'

'I don't think so.'

'What?' he said, putting on a laugh. 'It would just be a bit of fun.'

'No, it wouldn't,' I said, showing him the door.

'I wouldn't tell anyone.'

'I don't care,' I said, trying to mask how scared I was. I wasn't in the least bit interested in spending any time with James, and the thought of how ST would react if he thought anything had gone on was terrifying.

Eventually, he took the hint. But before he left he said, 'You'll regret this. Wait till he finds out about "us".'

I was relieved to see the back of him, but just as I was reflecting on how weird that experience was, two police officers arrived at the door to tell me the whereabouts of ST.

'He is currently being detained in prison,' they said. They could see the shock in my eyes. They explained that he had been pulled over for speeding, and once they ran their checks and discovered he was breaching his bail conditions they arrested him. He then appeared in court and was sentenced to eight weeks in prison. 'He is currently in HMP Swansea,' they said.

Once I knew where he was I left the cottage and moved back to my parents' house, but I knew it would only be temporary. Leaving him permanently was never an option. In just a few weeks he would be out. I believed he would murder me or my family if I tried to leave him. I was in a big hole and there was no escape. He would never let me go.

So it proved. A day or so later he called me from prison. He was furious about being locked up and was ranting about the police and how unfairly he'd been treated. Even though he was at the end of the telephone and banged up in prison, he still scared me.

After a few minutes he calmed down and his voice softened. 'I can't bear being apart from you, Sophie,' he said. 'It's tearing me apart. Will you come and visit me?'

It was about the nicest he had been to me. He said his mum would bring me, so I didn't really have an option.

We went a few days later. His mum told me she was a born-again Christian, but she sounded just like him in the way she let rip against the authorities, complaining about how she and her son had been treated.

As soon as we got through security to the visitors' area he came bounding up. He put his arms around me.

'Oi! Stop that!' A security guard was on him like a shot, telling us, 'No touching.'

ST looked like he was about to kick off, but he soon settled down.

'I hate it in here,' he said. 'You can't believe how terrible it is. And do you know the worst thing about it? Being apart from you. I miss you so much you wouldn't believe.'

His mum drove me home but that night he called me from prison. I thought he would gush more about how much he loved and missed me. Instead, he said, 'I wish you hadn't come to see me. I saw the way the guards were looking at you. I bet you all had an orgy the moment I was gone.'

It was a ridiculous suggestion, but he was serious. I couldn't believe someone could be so obsessed with sex.

His return home was an explosion of pent-up sexual frustration. He demanded sex from the moment he walked in the door. Without warning, he picked me up, like some caveman, and carried me upstairs. He threw me on the bed and pinned me down, his hands tight around my neck, releasing his grip only to grab my head in his meaty hands, screaming into my face, growling like a lust-crazed beast and forcing his thumbs into my eyes. He took huge chunks of my hair and pulled so hard it felt like it would rip out in clumps. He sank his teeth into my shoulders and bit my breast.

He panted, 'I've missed you. I love you. I want you.'

I just lay there, willing it all to end, already yearning for the days when he was behind bars and couldn't hurt me.

When it was finally over there was barely time to recover before he demanded more. I didn't think it possible that he could be even more sex-crazed, but his time away had pushed him to another level.

I also didn't think he could be any more disgusting. His personal-hygiene regime was already practically non-existent. It was a far cry from the time he came to the Socialist Party meetings and to my house in freshly washed clothes, smelling of aftershave. The longer I knew him, the less he washed. This was at complete odds with my OCD and passion for cleanliness. He used to mock me for being too clean, while he went days without taking a shower or washing.

But when he returned from prison he was filthier than ever. In the days following his release I started scratching. My whole body seemed to itch. He was scratching too. As the days wore on there was no respite. It felt like my whole body was alive. I soon discovered that he had brought back human fleas from prison. As someone who takes pride in cleanliness, this was anathema to me. I got treatment and tried to scrub the house clean, but they were everywhere. It was a mammoth task to get rid of them.

In those first days after his release he kept telling me he loved me, that he worshipped me and he wanted us to be together forever, yet his actions told a different story. After each sordid sex session I counted the new scars and worked out which clothes I could wear to hide the evidence. As I gingerly replaced another bra he'd broken while tearing it from me, and fastened it carefully over the scars and carpet burns, I asked myself whether this was all normal, like he said. And if it was all normal, I wondered why I felt so ashamed and embarrassed, and why I had to hide and cover up innumerable wounds. Was every woman doing the same? Hiding their shame? Were we all walking around behind a mask of respectability?

I yearned for those times when I was an innocent child and had my mother's nightdress as a comfort. Back then I lived in fear of things I couldn't control. Now, in some ways, nothing had changed. I still lived in fear. I lived with something I could not control.

I started going back to liking things that I'd enjoyed as a child. I hadn't watched the Disney movie *The Little Mermaid* since I was a kid, but one night, when he seemed out of it and was snoring loudly, I crept out of bed, went downstairs and put it on. Watching it for a few minutes made me feel so much better, transporting me back to a deeply troubled but, compared to this, much happier, simpler time. From then on, when I was awake in the middle of the night and I thought he wouldn't catch me, I'd sneak down and rewatch all the Disney classics, wishing I had a time machine and that I could be that little girl again, sleeping with my mammy and having her sing to me. For the briefest of moments I would be back there: in the darkness, feeling her soft touch, sensing her warm, soothing breath on the back of my neck as she lay with me. But then, just as quickly as the sensation arrived, it would be gone, and I'd sit there on the sofa realising that I would never get those moments back. Tears would fill my eyes and I'd know it was time to switch the movie off and retreat back upstairs before I was discovered.

Somewhere along the way things had gone so wrong; I just wished I could change them. I slid into bed wondering how things had changed so much, so fast and so horribly, and how the world was such a cruel, twisted place.

The demands for a baby were almost as constant as the demands for sex. With Star gone from our lives, children were very much back on the agenda. Without contraception, I was still at the mercy of nature. Given that he was limiting the food I ate to make me as skinny as a young child, it would probably have been a miracle if I did conceive, but that wasn't enough to stop me praying each month that my period would come. I thought that was my lifeline.

Until one day, when he'd forced himself upon me once more and noticed I was bleeding down below.

'Is that me?' he said triumphantly.

It took me a moment to work out what he meant. He was desperate to make me bleed. I told him it was my period.

His tone suddenly changed. 'Who have you been fucking?'

'What?'

'That,' he said, eyes darkening. 'Who are you having an affair with? I bet when I was inside you were having it off with all sorts.'

This was insane. I hardly ever left the house without him, and even when he was in prison I stayed at my parents', scared to leave the house in case I was out when he called.

I hurried down to the bathroom to clean myself up.

'Whoever it is must be big,' he shouted after me, following me downstairs.

Even the suggestion was disgusting. I hoped he might be joking, but when he bounded into the bathroom behind me I could tell he was adamant.

'It's my period,' I said again.

'Bullshit. You've been seeing someone else.'

I tried to back away but I was hemmed in against the bath. He filled the entire space. I could smell his foul breath. 'I want to be the only one who makes you bleed down there.'

'Don't be stupid,' I said, instantly regretting the words the moment they left my mouth.

'Who are you calling stupid, you lying bitch?' He grabbed me by the throat.

'I'm sor–'

I didn't get to finish the sentence. The slap he delivered to the side of my head was so powerful it felt like my brain was dislodged. I fell onto the toilet, mind spinning.

He dragged me into the living room and grabbed my phone. 'Show me who you've been in contact with.'

'No one,' I whimpered.

'You're a liar. You're screwing someone else. You always have been.'

'It's my period.'

He went tearing through the house, going through my things as if he was going to find evidence of an affair. I tried to work out where he was getting it from. Was it his relative James? He had vowed to make me pay for rejecting his advances. Was this his idea of payback – making up lies about me, probably knowing it would send ST berserk? I didn't know. I didn't have time to think about it further as he came up, stomping towards me with a crazed look on his face.

'You must be screwing the spirits, then?' he spat.

'What?'

'You know. You're so psychic, have you been having sex with spirits behind my back?'

I just shook my head. It was still throbbing. There was no point trying to reason with him.

'I'm going to see my mum,' I said.

'Liar! Just admit you're going to see your other man.' He grabbed his jacket and stormed out of the house, slamming the door behind him.

I put on a long-sleeved top to cover the marks on my arm from where he had grabbed me and went to see my parents. I expected to be pestered by his texts and calls, as was usual when I left him, but this time he was silent. He had left in such a rush that he had forgotten to take his phone, and I suspected he was staying out brooding somewhere. It was dark by the time I went back to the cottage. I was walking down the lane to our door when a black figure in a balaclava leapt out in front of me. I caught a flash of steel. Oh my God! It was a knife.

'Where have you been?!' the masked man growled.

It was him. What the hell? He'd nearly given me a heart attack.

'Where have you been?' He waved the knife – which I could now see was a huge Rambo-style hunting blade with a serrated edge – inches from my face.

'At Mum's. Like I told you.'

Had he been following me, waiting here all this time to pounce? I wouldn't have put anything past him. He grabbed me and manhandled me into the house, where he ripped off his balaclava but was still brandishing the knife.

'Who have you been having sex with?'

'No one! I've been at my mum's. I told you.'

He paced the room like a demented caged animal, tapping the blade on his palm, as though weighing up his options. I tried to remain calm, even though my heart was bursting through my chest. If he had followed me, he must have known I was telling the truth.

'Stop it, you're scaring me,' I said.

'Good,' he said, still pacing.

'I need to pee,' I said, hoping that putting a wall between us might make him calm down.

'You're not going anywhere,' he yelled.

'Please. I need to.' I moved towards the bathroom door.

'Bitch!' he screamed as he threw me into the wall. My face and right side took the full brunt of it – I felt a searing pain shooting down my arm and hip. I staggered to my feet. He slapped me over the ear. I thought my eardrum had burst, as I could suddenly only hear on one side.

'Stop!' I shouted.

He picked me up and pushed me through to the living room, screaming in my good ear, 'Liar! Bitch!'

I cowered on the sofa, my head throbbing, arm cut.

He stood over me yelling abuse. 'You're breaking my heart … you're evil … you're sleeping around … it's torturing me!'

He was going berserk. I thought it would never end. On and on he screamed about how evil and what a liar I was. During the tirade my ear popped. Now I had his verbal assault in stereo, but at least I wasn't going to be permanently deaf.

I curled up tighter and didn't utter a word as he ranted on, searching for new insults to hurl at me. I braced myself for more blows, but when none came I slowly began to have some clarity. I had to get out. I had to find the strength to stand up and leave. I thought of home, just two streets away. So close, yet so far. It didn't have to be this way. The first opportunity, I told myself, I would make a break for it.

Eventually, after nearly two hours of ranting, he finally stopped yelling. The silence was beautiful. I waited for him to leave the room before I slowly uncurled. Every limb ached. My head thumped and I'd have to patch up my arm once more.

I didn't care, though. Like a newborn deer trying to stand for the first time, I rose unsteadily to my feet. I listened for sounds of him returning. When none came I moved towards the door. One step at a time. Reaching the door, I turned the handle as quietly as possible.

I kept waiting for him to come crashing into the kitchen, to start screaming in my face and drag me by the hair to the bedroom. The door was ajar and still he hadn't arrived. I slipped out into the night and, limping heavily, moved as fast as I could to the end of the lane and turned the corner.

In just a few seconds I would be home – where I'd find sanctuary at last.

Chapter 12

The calls and texts began the moment I walked in the door.

'Where the fuck are you?'

'What do you think you are doing?'

'Get home now.'

My instinct was to reply straight away. If I didn't, the consequences would be brutal. Did I have to respond? What was this? An end to the violence? Or a temporary pause?

I closed down my phone. A reply could wait.

My parents were pleased to have me back in the house, but at the same time they were concerned for my well-being. They could tell I was suffering. I couldn't let on what had happened, though. It was too embarrassing. To do so would be acknowledging that it was wrong and I was in way too deep.

'We just need a break from each other,' I said.

I had been existing on two levels for what felt like forever – terrified every moment I spent with him but putting on a front to my family. I'd become good at it.

I switched my phone to silent but it buzzed incessantly. He was obviously furious at my insubordination. I imagined him in the cottage, getting out of his head on cannabis, brooding and plotting.

I went to bed that night relieved that, for the first time in months, I would not be subjected to a horrifying sexual assault. I had a meal in my stomach that I had been able to eat without someone commenting on how fat it would make me. I would be able to wear pyjamas – he insisted on me being naked in bed – and I would be warm and safe. There would be no one yelling in my face, my body would be spared any new pain. But although I lay down, relieved at the respite, my mind could not switch off. In the dark my body tensed, as though at any moment he would barge into my room, rip back the bed clothes and attack me. When I closed my eyes I could see him leering over me, the weight of his bulky frame crushing my tiny form. I could feel myself gasping for air.

When the phone buzzed for what must have been the fiftieth time since I'd left the house, I jumped like I hadn't heard it in months.

'Bitch.'

'You'll pay for this.'

I started shaking. Unable to sleep, I got up and carefully peered out of the window. The street was quiet, but what was that moving in the shadows thrown by the street lights? Was it him – standing outside, staring? It was hard to tell. It wouldn't have surprised me. He knew full well where I was. As I looked up and down the street I could see him lurking in every shadow.

I returned to my phone. 'I need to be alone,' I texted, and put the phone on silent before the inevitable response. I climbed back into bed and spent a fitful night replaying the horrors over and over in my head.

In the morning I got up to dozens of missed calls and unanswered texts, each more cruel and chilling than the last.

'Are you back to say goodbye to your dad?'

'He will soon be dead.'

'You will be dead too if you don't come back.'

What should I do? If I stayed away, who knew what he might do? But if I went back I knew what would be waiting for me. I was completely torn. A huge part of me never wanted to see him again, but it wasn't that easy, particularly with the never-ending calls, texts and now emails. He was like a man possessed.

I was paralysed. I didn't know what to do. I tried to reassure him that I would be back soon, while at the same time telling my parents I wouldn't go back. I stayed another night but, like before, I couldn't sleep for worrying about the consequences. His tone became even more threatening. In the middle of the night I looked out again. At first I thought I was imagining things again, but then I caught a glimpse of movement in the shadows and a figure emerged into the glow of the streetlight. It was him! It was 3 a.m. How long had he been standing there? I hid behind the curtain, terrified he might have seen me.

My phone buzzed: 'I'm watching you.'

The following day his tone became more desperate. I was breaking his heart. He couldn't live without me. He loved me more than life itself. I needed to be with him. We were destined to be together. Why was I punishing him this way? Why was I being so evil?

'I worship you, Sophie,' he said in one text. 'I want to kiss the very ground you walk on.'

It was too much for me to handle, but my parents implored me to stay. I stuck it out for a few more nights, still unsure of exactly what it was I was doing. It was impossible to relax. Since meeting him I hadn't read a book. He had forbidden it. The insatiable desire for knowledge I'd once had was a distant memory. Whereas once I was able to soothe my fevered mind with a host of interests, now I just sat there, unable to relax, my nerves shot to pieces. I was a shadow of the high-functioning, inquisitive child who had baffled experts. When I looked in the mirror I barely recognised the face staring blankly back.

I cursed my condition for skewing my mind. I wished I could fathom relationships and rationalise people's behaviour. It had always been so confusing for me. I wondered again if this was what a sexual relationship should be like. I had no way of knowing, and with the way my brain was wired it was unlikely I would ever be able to understand things like that. I had no idea what was normal and what was not.

I recalled, when I was three and struggling to fit in at nursery, being asked by one of the teachers what I wanted to be when I grew up. It seemed such a difficult question to answer – both then and now. I remember watching as the other children excitedly shouted out their answers – footballer, pop star. After giving it some thought I told the teacher I wanted to be an astronaut. Even at that tender age I liked the idea of leaving Earth, as it didn't feel like I fitted in. Fifteen years on, I felt the same way. Was there some way to leave this planet? Was there a way out of this world? Was there a place out there that accommodated someone like me? One that accepted my peculiarities rather than persecuting me for having them?

I had been there nearly a week when his tone changed again. He sent a flurry of texts.

'If I can't have you, Sophie, no one will.'

'Do you understand what I am saying? If you don't come back, I will kill you.'

'I'll kill you and your family.'

'I'll start with your poor sick dad.'

'I'm coming for you.'

I tried to reason with him over text but it was no good. The only thing he wanted to hear was that I was ending this stunt and returning to him.

If his threats hadn't been terrifying enough, his next made my blood freeze.

'This is it, Sophie. You have left me no choice. I'm going to burn your house down.'

I looked out of the window. Rain was lashing down. He was standing across the street. He was carrying something. To my horror, I saw it was a can of petrol. Oh my God, he was serious.

'I have to go,' I said to my parents. There was no way I could tell them why.

They couldn't understand that I had no choice. I was under his control. I could do nothing else.

'It's okay,' I replied to him. 'You don't have to do that. I'm coming back.'

With a leaden heart I left the sanctuary of my home and trudged the short route back to the cottage, resigned to whatever fate awaited me there.

Chapter 13

Entering the cottage for the first time in a week was like stepping back in time. The first thing that hit me was the smell of cannabis smoke, mixed with the foul stench of body odour and general grime. For a moment I thought I was back in his disgusting house. But something was different. It was dark in the kitchen, but from the living room came an eerie purple glow. It took me a while to work out that it was because the light bulbs had been changed to ultra-violet. As I looked around it was clear that he had not lifted a finger to clean or tidy the place while I had been away. Dirty clothes lay strewn on the floor, drug paraphernalia was everywhere.

He was clearly out of it. His eyes were glazed and manic, his hair long and greasy.

'What have you done?' I asked.

'It's cool, isn't it?' he said, looking around the place, before pulling me into a bear hug. 'We will never

177

be apart again. Never. Together forever. Together forever.'

He smothered me in kisses, pawing at my hair and body. 'I worship you, Sophie. I've missed you so much. Never do that to me again. Never.'

I knew what was coming.

'I want you now. I've missed you,' he said, over and over, as he picked me up and carried me upstairs. In the bedroom I braced myself for sex, but instead he forced me to pleasure him, pushing my head down so sharply I thought my neck would snap. I could tell he hadn't washed in the time I'd been away. He smelled foul and the thought of performing the sex act he wanted repulsed me. It was all I could do not to retch – I had to suppress every instinct in my body, which all my life had been sensitive to germs, filth and stench. All the time he kept groaning about how much he loved and missed me.

'I want us to be sewn together,' he said later, in bed, as he pulled my trembling, cold, naked body to his. 'I want to have constant contact. Never apart.' I spent the rest of the night pressed up against him.

In the morning he was still stuck to me like a leech. 'I need to go to the bathroom,' I said, trying to wriggle free.

'I'm coming with you.'

'You don't have to …'

He picked me up and carried me like a child down to the bathroom.

'Okay,' I said, when he put me down. 'You can leave me now.'

'I said we're going to be together all the time.' He stood there staring at me.

'I can't go with you here. Please. I'll only be five minutes.'

He shook his head. 'Together – all the time.'

My face was burning as I sat down. I couldn't believe this. Normally he only paid me attention when he wanted sex, which was constantly. But this was creepy. It took me an age to do my business with him staring at me. When I was done he continued to watch as I washed myself. Then he picked me up and carried me to the living room.

He placed me down on the sofa. I was shivering from the cold. I still had no clothes on.

'Please,' I said. 'Can I just get dressed?'

'Look,' he said, pointing to the large mirror hanging on the wall.

I noticed he had scrawled all over it in marker pen.

'Read it,' he said. 'It's all about togetherness.'

I had to read and re-read it slowly for it to register. It could only be described as a lecture on 'togetherness'; how spending seconds apart added up to hours and days over a lifetime; how together we were stronger and we would never be apart. As I tried to take it in he gave me a verbal rundown. This wasn't a vow or an endearing set of commitments. It was like a sermon. Thou shalt do what I want. Even after everything I'd been through, I had a deep sense of foreboding as to what this all meant.

After he was done with his lecture he picked me up again and carried me back upstairs.

'I can manage by myself,' I said, trying to summon a laugh – as though I was finding this all quite funny.

'You're not listening to me. I said I want to feel your contact *all* the time. I worship you, Sophie. This is how it has to be. I don't want to be apart from you for one second.'

He took me back into the bedroom and put me down on the bed. I got up to get some clothes but he pushed me back down. He then rummaged through my clothes and handed me a dress and some underwear.

'Wear this.'

'But I wanted to wear jeans today,' I said.

'I said wear that.' His eyes narrowed. 'Do I have to go over what I mean by togetherness?'

I shook my head and took the dress. As soon as my clothes were on he picked me up again, carrying me on his hip like a mother does a toddler, and down the stairs we went. In the kitchen he made breakfast for one, carried me to the sofa and spoon-fed me from his bowl while I sat on his lap. I was three stone short of my ideal weight – in his eyes – of four stone, but given that he was sixteen stone and over six foot, it was effortless for him to scoop me up.

'You need to put me down,' I said, when we were finished.

'We are doing everything together,' he said. 'You are not leaving my side ever again.'

'I get that,' I said, trying hard to accept what he was saying. 'But I wanted to have a bath and wash my hair this morning.'

'That's fine. We'll do it together.'

Up again we went, through to the bathroom. He stripped me off and I stood there while he ran a bath. He bathed me and washed my hair. Throughout I thought, *Humour him, Sophie. This is a phase. He will get bored eventually.*

So I played along. He carried me back to the living room, where he held me on the sofa on his lap. When he wanted to play games on his computer he put me to one side but remained pressed up against me. I had to sit there. I started to need the toilet again but was afraid to get up or ask in case it prompted another lecture.

'You don't need to come with me,' I said, when I could hold on no longer. 'But I really need to go to the toilet.'

'We'll go together.'

'No. Really. I need to do a poo,' I said, cringing that I was even spelling this out. 'I'll be quick.'

'Together,' he growled.

He carried me through and placed me down, removing my pants and lowering me onto the pan.

'Please,' I said, shaking with the need to go and the sheer humiliation of it all.

'Anything you need to do, you do with me.'

He was not going to leave. I tried to get it done as quickly as possible. Before I had finished he started undoing his trousers.

'What are you doing?' I tried to hide the horror in my eyes.

'I need to go too. Sit still. Spread your legs wider.'

I did as I was told, trying not to retch as he urinated in the space between my legs. When he was done he shook himself dry and waited until I'd finished before carrying me back to the sofa.

He is punishing me, I thought. *This is his revenge for my leaving the cottage for a week. It's a deliberate ploy. No one can be this deranged that they want to live like this. Can they?*

For the rest of the day he continued the 'togetherness' mantra. My feet hardly touched the ground. When he watched his sick porn he pulled me onto his lap and I could feel him getting aroused. He carried me upstairs, and during the inevitable rough sex constantly moved me around, barking orders: 'Do this, move that way, not like that – this way.'

As he tossed me around like a little ragdoll, I said to myself over and over again, *This won't last forever. It will be over soon.*

After another night of holding me tightly to him, there was no sign that he was tiring of his game. He selected my outfit – together with a bow for my hair – took me to the bathroom, spoon-fed me breakfast.

'No walls will ever come between us,' he said, when we left the bathroom. 'We will be together 24/7. We will die together.'

I thought some respite might come when his relative James turned up. Even though I detested him and suspected he was making life even worse for me, the fact that he was a stoner too led me to hope they would get wasted together and forget about me. I couldn't see him continuing this obsessive 'togetherness' tirade in front of someone else. He and James got high while playing loud music and watching sex channels. He forced me to sit with them and forbade me to leave the room. It was excruciating, watching them guffaw over pornographic films in which women used as sex dolls were expected to be grateful that several men wanted to have sex with them at the same time.

I felt affinity with the women in these films. Despite their moans of ecstasy, they looked dead behind the eyes. They were going through the motions, empty vessels there purely for male gratification. Just as he strived to emulate the male stars of these films with his sexual appetite, while feeling inadequate against the freakishly big men who featured in them, so too was I playing the part of the brainless sex dolls. What amazing actresses we were.

I could only watch for so long, though. Not only did I find them repulsive, but my head throbbed from the ultra-violet glow. He forbade me from reading books, but in this oppressive light I wouldn't have been able to complete a page without my eyes aching.

Why was this happening to me? What had I done to deserve a life like this?

James left, and not long after we had another visitor – his mum. She had been in touch with him a lot more since his spell in prison. She happened to mention that Luke had a new carer. Something in the way they talked about that little boy made me suspect he wasn't his cousin, as he'd told me previously.

'Who is Luke?' I asked him, after his mother had left.

'My son,' he said, in a very matter-of-fact way.

I must have been unable to disguise the look on my face, as he went on to explain that he had two sons – there was an older one called Mark. Both were the products of a relationship he'd had a few years before meeting me. It was unusual for him to be so open. He explained that since he'd split from the boys' mother, social services had tried to stop him from having any contact with them or her.

He blamed the lack of contact on his ex. He said he left her because he got bored – and he hated her.

Hearing about his background worried me. I didn't understand at first. I thought that maybe social services had jumped to conclusions and removed the children as a precaution, but I knew so very little about this man, how did I know that what he was telling me now was the truth? What would his ex have to say about why he couldn't see his own children?

How much could I believe about anything he had told me? He had never really talked about his childhood, just about his dog, which I didn't believe he ever had, given the way he'd treated Star.

I asked him about his childhood. He said he had been expelled from a number of different comprehensive schools, which was why he held no formal qualifications. This could well have been true, but what could he have done to get expelled from different schools? Would I ever find out the truth about him?

After a while he shut the conversation down and returned to his theme of 'togetherness'. He sat me on his lap and pawed at my skin. He ran his hands through my hair. 'I bet you'd look gorgeous bald,' he said, tugging at my hair. 'It would be so sexy.'

I stayed silent, trying to work out where this was going.

'We could be bald together,' he said. 'It would mark us out as one.'

He got up, went into the kitchen and returned with a pair of scissors.

'What are they for?' I asked, starting to tense up.

'For cutting off my hair.'

I laughed nervously. 'You're not serious.'

He wasn't laughing. 'I want us both to be bald.' He handed me the scissors. 'Go on. Do it.'

'I don't want to,' I said.

'Do you not love me, Sophie?' The way he was holding the scissors, blades pointing to my chest, I feared he would stab me if I didn't give him the answer he wanted.

'Of course I do.'

'Then cut off my hair.' He offered the scissors to me once more. I took them.

'I love you. You don't understand. I worship you.' His eyes were glazed. He was clearly out of it. 'I want to be you. If I can't be you then the next best thing is to be next to you, always – to look like you.'

I started trimming locks of his hair.

'More! Cut it all off!' he shouted, when he felt I was taking too long and being too careful. Soon the living-room floor was covered with locks of dark hair. I cut it as close as I could.

'I'm going to buy a razor,' he said. 'For you. We'll shave both our heads. You'll look so sexy. I can't wait to come on your bald head.'

I shuddered. He could not be serious.

He got his laptop and looked up electric hair-trimmers on eBay. When he found one he liked he ordered it and showed me. He seemed pleased with himself. At night, as he held me tightly to him, I prayed that by morning he'd have forgotten all about it.

I was not allowed out of the house on my own, so everything we did, we did together. In a couple of the local shops remarks were made by the women who worked there on how short his hair was.

'Sophie did it while I was sleeping,' he said. 'I didn't ask her. She just did it.'

There was no point challenging him. I just smiled and held my tongue.

When we returned to the house he played games on his computer while I had to sit by his side. He preferred me to do nothing but there was one activity he allowed. He'd loved the idea of me collecting dolls when I was younger. It made me seem more childlike in his eyes. When I told him I liked making ragdolls he encouraged me. And so I'd sit there, eyes straining in the sinister ultra-violet light, stitching together little dolls. They were all sad, like characters from *The Nightmare Before Christmas*. A favourite was one with long dark hair, black button eyes and a stitched, downturned mouth. I dressed her in a white top, her arms tight to her chest, as though trussed up in a straitjacket. Black ragged trousers completed her outfit. I told myself that this couldn't get any worse. I just had to get through it.

You are me, I thought, when I'd finished making her. A ragdoll, to be tossed around at will, with no thoughts in your head and no life of your own.

His possessiveness became so complete, the only respite I had was when he slept and I lay awake, relishing the hours of darkness, free of his constant abuse.

I started to write down thoughts and stories, trying desperately to articulate what I was thinking, hoping my imagination might set me free. All that came out, however, were dark thoughts that mirrored reality.

One such story was 'The Fly', which I wrote during a brief moment of respite. It gives an idea of how I was feeling:

Darkness descended onto the bedroom, night was fast approaching. I closed the curtains, prepared the bed, ready to have a long and peaceful sleep.

My head rested against the soft duck-feather-and-down pillow, my eyes slowly started to close and I could feel myself drifting to the land of imagination, when I suddenly heard a loud buzzing sound.

I opened my eyes, turned on the electric light and looked around the bedroom for the cause of this irritating noise, and there I saw it: a huge, black, dirty fly standing on the wall.

I rolled up a magazine, ready to end its life early, but, just as I launched at it, off it flew, buzzing away around the room.

It seemed like it was out of control. It flew around me, into my face, around my head. It would not land. I swatted it away with my hand and the buzzing stopped.

After about five minutes spent looking for the creature, I convinced myself that I must have been triumphant and killed the beast.

I knocked out the light and again laid down to rest.

I fell into a deep sleep. I did not know how much time had passed when again I heard the buzzing. That accursed fly.

I leapt out of bed, ready once again to battle with it. At first I couldn't see it. I could only hear the infernal buzzing, which felt like daggers piercing my brain.

'Where are you?' I shouted

I could still hear it, but it was nowhere to be seen.

My heart started to pound hard against my chest, my palms started to sweat, but the infernal buzzing continued.

I couldn't stick the noise, and the thought of that disgusting flying monster in my bedroom made me crazy. I needed to find it and rid the world of it.

I looked under the bed, scattering my books and shoes everywhere, but it wasn't there.

I threw off the cushions and bedclothes from the bed. They fell to the floor in a heap, but it wasn't there.

I opened my wardrobe and started frantically flinging clothing around the room until the wardrobe was empty, but again it wasn't there.

I felt like I was losing control. I pulled everything off the shelves. Ornaments smashed into a thousand pieces on the wooden floors. Still the buzzing continued, seemingly louder than before, like it was deliberately taunting me.

Maybe it has got behind the wallpaper, I thought to myself, so I started pulling the paper off the wall, ripping and tearing it. I felt like a wild beast going into frenzy, but I couldn't stop.

A few hours must have passed and all the wallpaper was now off the wall. No fly, but still it buzzed!

'Where are you, you bastard?' I shouted.

I ran down to the kitchen and grabbed a knife. *This will get it*, I thought.

Running back up the stairs, I fell and knocked my head. Blood poured down my face but I didn't feel it. I just wanted to kill that thing.

I approached the bedroom, calmly hiding the knife behind my back. I shut the bedroom door behind me and was greeted with the buzzing, but this time I saw it, rubbing its face with its disgusting legs. It had grown to enormous proportions.

Its bulging eyes staring at me, it turned its head. I seized my chance and lunged full force at it, throwing the knife against the wall, but the fly casually flew away. The knife missed it by mere inches.

I picked up the knife and started swirling it around my head. The fly then landed on me, right on my left leg. I lifted up the knife and swung it down, cutting through my flesh, but the beast then flew onto my right arm. Again, I swung the knife, this time embedding it into my flesh.

The blood poured out of me but I felt elated. I must have killed it. I cried in ecstasy. Then I heard the buzzing.

'No, it can't be!' I screamed.

Just then, my husband stood at the bedroom door, pale and trembling with fear. He

looked around the room with frightened eyes.
He saw the blood and spittle running down my
face.

'It's the beast. The fly. It's here. Listen to the
buzzing. The buzzing!'

He slammed the door and locked it from the
outside.

'It's not me, it's the fly!' I screamed, as I
punched on the door with all my might.

Hours seemed to pass, but in reality it must
have been minutes as I sat in delirium, leaning
against the door.

The fly still buzzed around me, but then I had
a marvellous idea. I couldn't believe that I had
not thought of this before.

What kills flies? Spiders, of course!

I closed my eyes and imagined myself turning.
I felt hair growing, felt myself sprouting
additional legs and eyes. I looked down at
myself and was greeted with the sight of eight
hairy legs.

'Now I will get you, you bastard' I laughed
hysterically. I crawled across the floor on my
newly grown legs and I seemed to be able to
climb the wall.

I went in pursuit of the fly, but it still kept
eluding me.

Just then, the door flew open. My husband stood there with five men in white coats.

'Stay back,' I screamed, 'or I will sting you!'

The next thing I knew, I was being tied up and loaded into the back of a van.

'The fly! The fly!' I screamed, as they pushed me into the van.

As they spirited me away, I looked up at my bedroom window to see the enormous black beast looking down at me. It grinned and waved.

Chapter 14

Now that he had control of my wardrobe, he increasingly dressed me in girly clothes, so I looked even younger. Between carrying me about, controlling my clothes, washing me and feeding me, I felt as helpless as a baby.

This was how he had always wanted me. And the more childlike I was, the more twisted his sexual desires became.

'Were you abused when you were younger?' he leered at me one night, while he had me on his lap on the sofa.

'No!'

'Come on. I bet you were. I can tell. Who did it? Who touched you up?'

'I was never abused.' The thought of it made my skin crawl. Why would he even think that? Although I had opened up about many aspects of my childhood, I hadn't said anything to make him think such a thing. It seemed to be something he just wished were true.

'You can tell me,' he persisted. It was like he was getting off on this. It must have been some sort of sick fantasy. 'You can tell me everything.' He pulled me closer. 'Did you enjoy it?'

I shook my head and tried to wriggle free of his grasp. He only held on tighter and moved his hand up my leg.

'Tell me you were abused ... was it when you were very young? Three or four?'

'It's sick to even think that,' I said.

'I wish I'd known you as a kid,' he breathed into my ear. 'I would have totally fucked you.'

My stomach churned. I felt sick in my mouth. But I said nothing, hoping he might get bored and want to get stoned or play on his computer.

'Pretend to me, then,' he said. 'Tell me what you wanted to happen.'

There was no way I was playing along with this. It was sick. But I'd lost so much of myself I wasn't in control of my mind anymore. Part of me felt that if he wanted to believe that then so be it. My resistance was falling away to nothing.

Whether I liked it or not, I had been under his control for months now. I lived for him, end of story. I went to bed when he went to bed, ate when he fed me, washed when he wanted me to wash. I was living for him, not myself. It was round-the-clock, constant control.

If that wasn't enough, I was living in near darkness, under UV-light, in a distorted reality. I didn't take drugs but at times I felt as spaced out as he was on cannabis. It was so oppressive, driving my mood down. My senses were dulled, my system felt like it was shutting down. The only things that were heightened were fear and paranoia.

I longed for the basic rights that people took for granted, like being able to go to the bathroom on my own. Since his 'togetherness' regime had kicked in, I'd grown scared of what the bathroom represented. When he slept I longed to go to the toilet but never dared for fear of what he would do if he caught me. It was getting to the point where I couldn't remember what it was like to go to the toilet unaccompanied. I started to worry that I'd never be able to go alone again.

I would hear the creaking of floorboards downstairs and convince myself that someone had broken in to attack us. I was returning to the scared little girl too frightened to go outside. The only difference was that now I was also scared to remain in the house. His overpowering control was suffocating, but as I sank lower into depression I sometimes wondered, *If he did leave the door open, would I run?* I felt like a laboratory rat, pushed, probed and tested to the point of submission, too conditioned to the cage to brave the outside world.

Being such a prisoner meant I was at the mercy of every whim and twisted perversion he wanted to practise. He still obsessively took thousands of photos. All of them of me – or us together, reinforcing his mantra.

It was weird seeing my face staring back at me from every shelf and wall, the colours distorted under the UV. And he didn't stop there.

I was naked in bed one day – a state I spent much of my life in – when he produced the camera. Even though I knew that trying to defy him was futile, I instinctively pulled the sheet over me.

'Let me take you naked,' he said, pulling the sheet back. 'It'll be erotic.'

I reached for the cover again. Taking photos of me at my most vulnerable did not seem right. It felt weird. Why would he want to do this?

'Let me,' he said, tugging once more at the sheet, camera at the ready. 'Don't be such a prude. It's perfectly normal. Couples do it all the time. Those that are in love, that is. You do love me, Sophie? Because if you loved me, you would do this for me.'

Was he telling the truth? Was this what regular couples did? I had no idea. My instinct was to resist, but I couldn't tell if this was my Asperger's at work or if I really should be concerned. It was impossible to tell.

'You want to make me happy, don't you, Sophie?' His tone was threatening now. 'You don't want me to be upset.'

The last thing I wanted was to make him angry. Anything was preferable to that, so I let go of the covers and did as he wanted. He snapped away, not content with one or two images. His photo session went on for hours. He took hundreds of shots. He ordered me to pose one way, then another, each position seeming more grotesque than the last. He took intimate shots of my private bits and demanded I pull faces and pout like I was a glamour model. I can't imagine that these were in any way erotic. I must have looked dead behind the eyes. That was certainly how I felt. I hated every second of it.

I had red marks on my skin from where his hands had gripped my neck, nearly strangling me during sex. He zoned in on these. They seemed to turn him on too. I also sported bruises on my arms and legs where he'd grabbed or pushed down on me. He photographed these too, from every angle.

As he looked through the images afterwards, I saw the same twisted look on his face that he had when he viewed his sick pornographic videos.

'Plenty of men would love to see these,' he said, scrolling through the hundreds of photos.

I often zoned out when he spoke because it was either

abhorrent or monotonous drivel coming out of his mouth, but when he said this my ears pricked up.

'What did you say?' My voice trembled.

'These photos of you. There are plenty of people out there who would love these.'

'You said they were private. You would be the only one who would ever see them. That was what you said.'

He shrugged. 'That was before I saw how good they are. These are hot. You look stunning. Better than anything else you see out there.'

I shuddered. He loaded the images onto his computer. Now I started to worry. Where would they end up? Was this for his own private collection, as he said, or was he going to post them on the Internet somewhere? He knew so much about the Dark Net, the images could be anywhere and I'd never know.

'You know there are people who pimp out their wives?' he said, while he was still viewing the pictures. 'Would you like that? Would you like me to traffic you out? Imagine that. Men paying to fuck you. Would you like that? You'd do well. Men would be queuing up. You'd like that, wouldn't you?'

I shook my head. What made him think like this? It surely wasn't normal. For someone who had made such a big deal about me supposedly having affairs – with the living and the dead – why would he want to entertain the thought of me having sex with strangers?

'I could put these online,' he said, 'post requests and see what response I get. I bet it would be huge. You'd do well, you know.'

He smiled but I couldn't tell if he was joking or not. I wouldn't have put it past him to post the images on the net. It was like he was fine with me sleeping with other people but only on his conditions. Was it all part of his control?

I could only wait to find out. Like his desire to shave my head, I was at the mercy of forces outside my control. The only thing that had stopped him making me bald was that the clippers he'd ordered hadn't arrived. Perhaps my prayers were being answered after all.

This was my life now. Every day presented a new horror – something to feel terrified about. Something I had to pray wouldn't get worse. These episodes had become part of life – just another example of the weird or perverted becoming the norm.

He was like a cancer, I thought to myself when I lay awake at night and he lay snoring beside me – a temporary respite. He was a cancer eating away at me, killing me from the inside, destroying my healthy cells, breaking me down piece by piece, moving from organ to organ. He was in my blood, my brain and my heart. There was no cure, no remedy. Nothing to ease the pain. I was terminally ill. Did I have years, months, weeks left? Who could tell? I could see no end to it. I could never leave him. He knew that. He knew he had total control. The thought of me leaving him never entered his head.

But was there another way? Some way to escape this living hell? As my grip on reality loosened I started to think that maybe there was a way to end it. I would prefer something quick and total – something there was no coming back from. I fantasised about the possibilities. I could jump in front of a train. That would be quick. There would be no chance of resuscitation, no prospect of being returned to this hellish existence. I could take an overdose but that would be risky. It might not be total, and I'd have to live with the consequences if I didn't do the job properly.

It was this bad. I just wanted to get out and get rid of him, and the only way I could see that happening was by taking my own life … or I could take his.

That was another fantasy. I had visions of smashing him over the head with something when he was out of it on cannabis. What would I use? What would be heavy enough to do the job? Would I be able to whack him hard enough? One blow would be ideal. If I had to rain down blow after blow, would he wake up? What then? He was so much bigger than me. He would easily overpower me. And then he would kill me. Without hesitation. He would do to me whatever I was trying to do to him.

Would I be able to give him an overdose? I could crush up some medication and put it in his food. Get some rat poison. It was all fanciful. It was impossible, given that I was never allowed to leave the house alone. Nevertheless, thoughts like this gave me great pleasure. I wouldn't have regretted killing him. Not one bit. Of that I was sure.

Maybe it wouldn't come to that. Maybe someone was watching over me who would deliver me from this evil. If they were, though, they had a strange way of showing it.

Chapter 15

'Go on, Sophie, just do it.' He was getting agitated with me.

'I can't. It's not right.' My hands were sweaty. I looked around. I was sure everyone was watching me. They all knew what I was about to do.

'You're making us look suspicious by messing around. Just put it in your bag and act casual. And do it now!'

We were in a large supermarket in Aberdare. I thought we were there for food but he had other ideas. It was only when he'd directed me to the electrical goods that he revealed what he wanted me to do: steal for him.

I stood there with the memory card in my hand. I had already ripped the security tag off so the alarm wouldn't go off, but the act of actually putting it in my bag was so much harder. It wasn't right. Stealing was wrong. What if I got caught? It would be me in trouble.

'Get fucking on with it,' he spat, pretending to look at some other items nearby.

God, was this what I had become? My life was well and truly not my own.

I dropped it into my bag. 'Okay, let's go,' I said.

'Nice one,' he whispered.

We headed for the door, passed the scanners and the security desk, and got outside.

'See, I told you it was easy.'

'That was awful,' I said. I could feel my heart pounding. I had never broken the law before, even on someone else's orders. It wasn't a nice feeling.

We were in this situation because the money was gone. He had wasted all my compensation – money that had been sitting, earning, until I was old enough to spend it responsibly. His last major expenditure was a new car – a black Suzuki Jimny off-roader with a detachable sunroof. Another toy for him to play with. But after that there was nothing left.

Now his plan was to steal items that could be sold on eBay. He needed the money to fund his drug habit and pay for a new laptop. He bragged to me about all the stuff he'd managed to steal over the years and how easy it was. He said he'd made thousands of pounds that way. Since getting his hands on my cash he hadn't needed to steal. And now that he had me, he didn't have to do it himself anymore.

He was pleased we'd got away with the memory card. Now he wanted me to steal more. He took me back to the shop. I expected us to return to the same aisle, but he had a different target in mind. He led me to the larger electrical items and pointed at a set of designer hair-straighteners.

'We'll get much more for these,' he said.

'I can't take that. It's huge. It'll set off the alarm for sure.'

'What did I say?' he hissed. 'Do it quickly and casually and no one will get suspicious. The longer you hang about and make a fuss, the more attention you get.'

I glanced around. Other shoppers were idly browsing or otherwise on a mission and checking items off a list. A couple of people clocked me looking at them. *They must know*, I thought. It must have been obvious that I was about to do something criminal.

'Get on with it!'

I picked up the box and, under the pretext of looking to see all the features, found the security tag and tore if off. I then dropped the box into my large bag.

As we walked to the door he peeled off so that he wasn't next to me as I exited. Nice. Leave me to get the blame. Again, I walked out unmolested. Surprisingly, it did seem as easy as he'd said.

From that day, he was obsessed. The laptop he wanted was £2,000, but there were other gadgets he needed –

boys' toys, I called them – and he was desperate to get them all as quickly as possible. I thought we were asking for trouble. We went from shop to shop, stealing a whole host of technological devices. I am not a tech person and I didn't know what a lot of the stuff was, but I knew the items were expensive. Each time I was the one wearing the bag. He would often put them in the bag, but if we got caught I'd be the one prosecuted because I was carrying everything. At one point there were thousands of pounds in the PayPal account, all from shoplifted stuff.

No one was on to us. Or so I thought.

We were walking out of one supermarket when I heard a voice behind me: 'Excuse me, madam.' There was a hand on my shoulder. 'Do you mind coming this way, please?'

It was a store security guard. *Oh no*, I thought, *we are in trouble now*. I started to sweat. Suddenly, ST was beside me. He didn't seem bothered at all. The security guard took us over to the desk and asked to see what was in my bag. I had no option but to show him. I can't even remember what it was. All I was thinking about was what I would say to the police – and that I wanted to be away from there.

To my astonishment, the guard seemed to know ST and he hadn't requested any other members of staff to help him. It was like the guard was frightened of him. ST was a big man, broad as well as tall, and naturally strong. At his old house I'd seen him break a piece of wood with his hands, which were larger than my head. Compared to the security guard he was a giant. The guard just confiscated the goods, told us not to do it again or he'd call the police, and let us go on our way.

'Come on,' ST said, as he grabbed me by the arm and led me out to the waiting car. I scurried alongside, trying to keep up, my mind spinning with the implications of what had just happened. If people in authority thought twice about prosecuting him, what chance would I ever have?

He seemed to be untouchable. He could drive like a maniac and never be stopped. He could steal things, get caught and nothing was done.

His next target was a carbon-monoxide alarm. Apparently, they had a good resale value. He thought a DIY store in Pontypridd was fair game. By this time he was so blasé it was a wonder he even bothered concealing the item. We were leaving the store and my thoughts were already turning to where he'd target next week when I caught sight of a man approaching. It was a security guard, a pretty burly one at that, dressed all in black. He was reaching for his radio.

'Excuse me, you two,' he said, just as we were almost through the door. That was all he managed to say.

ST suddenly turned and, before he was even challenged, went crazy and kicked the guard in the stomach with his big steel-toe-capped boots. The man doubled over. That would have hurt. People were standing, staring, but this wasn't the time to hang about.

'Run!' he shouted, and sprinted off to the Jimny. I ran after him and had just managed to climb in when he started the engine and took off across the car park, the doors still swinging open. A massive crowd of people had now gathered to see what the commotion was, and they stood, stunned, as we careered out of the car park and onto the road. It was a miracle we didn't hit another car or pedestrian as he screeched round bends like the getaway driver in a movie. It was insane. More than once I was convinced that the car was going to tip over. I was hanging on for dear life.

He slowed down enough to shut the doors and then we were off again, bombing it out of the town and heading up to the mountains. He eventually found a secluded spot and slammed on the brakes. He jumped out of the car and was still going mental, ranting and raving about the security guard.

'He attacked me. You saw that, right? I was only defending myself. He deserved what he got. I'm not standing for this shit. I'm not going down for that fucker. I hope I've ruptured his intestines.'

He paced around like a lunatic, shouting and bawling. Inevitably, he homed in on me.

'It's all your fault of course,' he said. 'You fucked it all up. It's your fault he was on to us. Why can't you be more savvy? You've done it this time. You stupid idiot.'

Then he started to panic about what might happen once the police started their investigation. No doubt there was CCTV in the shop, and if they had cameras in the car park it wouldn't take them long to trace the car.

'I'm fucked. This is it for me. They'll send me to jail. I'm done for.' Round and round he paced, still ranting. 'I'll leave the country. That's it. I'll fuck off where no one will find me. That will show them.'

There was no point trying to reason with him. He was like a man possessed. Eventually, though, he calmed down enough to get back in the car and drive down the mountain.

'I need to get rid of the car,' he said, once we were back in the cottage. 'That's the thing that will trace it back to us. I'll sell it tomorrow.'

For once, he was as good as his word. In a few days the car was gone. He thought he'd cracked it then, that he was one step ahead of the law. He didn't think the police would find him.

He was stunned when two police officers showed up at the cottage a couple of days later. He looked shocked and I could tell from his eyes that he was furious he'd been caught, but I was also amazed to see him turn on the charm. He called them both 'officer' all the time and denied knowing what they were talking about, but said he wanted to cooperate as much as possible. He had a tone to his voice that took me a while to recognise. Then I realised. It was how he was when we first met, all upbeat and nice. I had almost forgotten he could be like that. I found it interesting to watch him in front of authority figures. He was diminished somewhat, not quite the same imposing character he was with me. The officers asked me some questions about the incident, but I just lowered my head and muttered one-word answers into my chest. They didn't push me on it. I got the feeling that they realised I wasn't going to confirm anything that might land him in trouble. I even wondered if they felt sorry for me.

A court date was fixed, and in the run-up to it his personality changed. He had always liked to maintain that he lived by his own set of rules and he could handle anything, but I watched him change from this arrogant individual into a nervous wreck. He was fretting about going to court and what it would mean when he was convicted.

'You don't understand,' he said, when he was getting worked up about it. 'I've been to prison before. I know how bad it is. I can't go back there but there's no way I'll escape it. They'll definitely send me down for this.'

Seeing him so agitated made me wonder who he really was. I realised that there was still so much I didn't know about this man I lived with.

The closer to the date it got, the more worried he became. Given that he couldn't bear to let me out of his sight, how would he cope with another imposed separation? He twisted his anxieties onto me, though.

'If I go to jail, who will look after you?' he asked. 'You need me. You can't cope on your own.'

I couldn't begin to process what his going to prison might mean. I listened to what he said and wondered if he was right. Maybe I wouldn't be able to cope. Who would be there to feed me and clothe me?

On the day of his appearance in court I could tell he was panicking, but he transferred it all onto me.

'I can see you're scared, Sophie, that you won't be able to cope without me,' he said, as he paced the room repeatedly, checking the clock and adjusting his clothes. 'Promise me you will write to me every day. I want to know what you are doing every minute of every day. I'll call you every chance I have.'

He maintained throughout that he wanted to plead not guilty and take his chances, but his solicitor advised him to change his plea. There were so many witnesses to the assault. He wanted me to accompany him to Pontypridd Magistrates' Court. I sat at the back of the courtroom.

He tendered his plea and presented a letter he said I'd written to court, which spelled out my various health issues, said I needed round-the-clock supervision and explained that he was my full-time carer. It said how devastated I would be if he was sent to prison. I never wrote a word of it. He'd penned it himself.

It didn't have the impact he was hoping for. The court sentenced him to 12 weeks in prison. I felt a surge of relief but then a creeping terror gripped me. Twelve weeks was not a long time. He might not even serve that long. Any thoughts of using this enforced break to leave him were pointless. There was no way I could do that. I still couldn't bring myself to tell my parents about the abuse I was suffering. It would only be a matter of time before he was back – and I remembered how he'd been the last time he returned home from a spell inside.

He turned to look at me from the dock. I forced myself to cry. I knew he would be studying my body language, and if I didn't seem devastated enough he would store it up for when he could exact his revenge.

He might have been gone, but I couldn't bear the thought of staying at the cottage. I could feel his presence everywhere. I moved back into my parents' house. Being back in my own room once again provided some blessed relief. For a fleeting moment I had some respite from the fear. Away from the oppressive darkness and UV light, I could breathe once more. I even felt inspired to reach for my pen and write some verses. In some, like one I called 'Silence', I tried to encapsulate my continued isolation, a state that now had some peace:

Against My Will

The rain taps on the window pane.
Sounding like gentle music to my listening ears.
I sit inactive, just listening to the rain beating
 down.
I am alone, the room is dark, but I am not sad,
 lonely or afraid.
For thy company is great, and silence apart from
 the rain is most greatly desired.

I should have known the respite wouldn't last. The prisons in Wales were at full capacity so he had to serve his sentence somewhere in England. It took a couple of days for him to get settled and then the phone calls came. It was like déjà vu – gushing, extreme proclamations of love morphing into bitter vows of vengeance against those who'd crossed him.

'Do you want me to come visit you?'

'No,' he said. I was surprised. I thought he'd demand it.

'Why not?'

'I don't want a repeat of last time,' he muttered. 'You'll just have sex with the prison guards – either in a great big orgy or they'll take turns to rape you.'

Comments like that made it feel like he was still around. He could poison any conversation.

He fired questions at me: 'What have you been doing? Tell me everything you've done since I last saw you.

What are you wearing? What are you eating? Write to me, tell me everything.'

I did as I was told and wrote him a long letter. He was calling me as often as three times a day, so it was hard to know what to write. He knew everything anyway. In a couple of days he phoned and said, 'Send me a letter every day telling me what you most miss about me. Tell me what you'd like me to do to you. Make them as sexy as possible. I miss you more than life itself. I can't bear to think of you without me being there.'

With nothing to do all day, his mind was working overtime, obsessing about me. Here was a person who wanted to be with me 24 hours a day, who accompanied me to the toilet, and now he was somehow going to have to cope for three months. He was going out of his mind. He couldn't cope being without me. He wasn't able to keep an eye on me 24 hours a day and it was driving him mad.

I sat down to do as I was told. How could I bring myself to write the things he wanted? I hated any sexual act he instigated with every fibre in my body. To write them down would be reliving every touch that had made my skin crawl, every moment he hurt me. It would remind me of every time I'd lain there wishing to God it was over and I could breathe again. Worse, though, was the fact that by writing such deviant sexual things in a letter I would be legitimising my suffering. It would be saying I liked it. That I wanted him to do those things to me again. I would be giving my consent to him treating me so horribly. My hand shook as I held the pen, as though it didn't want to carry out my brain's instructions. My stomach lurched at the thought of the effect it would have on him when he read it.

Yet not doing as he said wasn't worth thinking about. Failure to obey him would mean just as much sexual violence, but in addition the screaming, the insults, the threats, the slapping and pushing, the pulling of my hair. If I didn't write these letters he would be convinced that it was because I was sleeping around, getting my pleasure from someone else. And the repercussions when he got out of prison would be brutal.

So, against every instinct I had, I wrote out his sexual fantasies and gave life to his sickest desires. Only after I'd finished did I wonder if his mail was vetted in prison. Would some security officer be reading these, getting their own kicks, or laughing and showing them to their colleagues? Would the letters be confiscated and not even reach him? That would be unbearable. He'd never believe I sent them.

The prison mail-vetting system must not have been as rigorous as I'd feared, as two days later he called to say how much he loved my letters, but he wanted more – much more.

'Make them sexier,' he said. 'You're holding back. Tell me your darkest fantasies. We'll act them out when I get home.'

I shuddered. I lived in a perpetual state of unease and fear of his release.

His incessant calls continued. Once, he rang while my mother was in earshot, and he was screaming so loudly that she suddenly said, 'Put the phone down on him!'

She couldn't believe I would tolerate someone speaking to me like that. When I didn't hang up and instead sat there while he ranted on, she shook her head, unable to comprehend it. She didn't know that there was no way I could end the call. To do so would be suicide.

'You should be writing several letters,' he said to me. 'I want you to record every single thing you're doing, every hour of every day. I don't want to miss one second of your life while I'm stuck in here.'

He scribbled out letters to me in return, some equally explicit, while in others he professed his undying love. One, which he entitled 'All the reasons why I love you', he told me to put on my wall, so I did, thinking he would like to hear that. He did, but after a day or so I couldn't bear to look at it so I took it down, making out to him that I wanted it by my bedside instead.

'I'm counting the hours, minutes, seconds until I'm back with you, Sophie. I will be back there soon,' he said. 'And I will love you like never before.'

I too was counting the hours, minutes and seconds until his return – for entirely different reasons. I braced myself for what I thought life would be like for me when he came out.

I had no idea.

Chapter 16

On his release from prison I returned to the cottage. It was night-time and he was going through the letters we'd sent each other while he was inside – a massive pile on the sofa. He had been sleeping all day so he was wide awake, but I was very tired and wanted to go to bed. He was in quite a tender mood, unusually, and when I went to bed he kissed me and, for once, I felt myself slip into a sound sleep.

Could I dare to dream he'd come home a changed man?

An hour later I woke to feel him sitting on the bed, caressing my hand. He was staring into space. I smiled and thought how nice this was. He turned, and when he saw I was awake his expression suddenly darkened.

He grabbed me by the throat, squeezing tightly.

'You are a liar!' he screamed.

I was choking. I grabbed his wrist with both hands and tried to prise him off, but he was too strong. In his other hand he brandished a piece of paper. I could barely make it out, my eyes were watering so much as I gasped for breath.

He held it up in front of my eyes. It was a prison letter: 'All the reasons why I love you'.

'You said you'd stuck it on the wall. Why, then, can I not feel any Blu Tack mark?'

I had no idea. I'd definitely stuck it up in my old room.

'Bitch! I'm going to kill you!' He squeezed tighter.

I punched his arm to try to make him let go. I barely managed to mouth: 'I did. I did.'

He eased his grip but his hand remained poised.

I spluttered to life. 'I did,' I said. 'I promise.' My neck felt red raw.

'Liar!'

'I promise you, I did.'

'Then where's the evidence? Where's the mark?'

If I'd thought for one second he would look for proof I would have kept the Blu Tack on the letter. It never occurred to me.

'Please check again,' I sobbed. 'In the middle, at the top.'

He held the letter to the light, running his thumb gently over the paper.

'Hmmm,' he said eventually. 'Maybe you're right.'

He released the grip on my neck. Thank God. I gently rubbed my throat and took deep breaths to try to stave off a panic attack. He switched off the light and left the room. There was no way I could go back to sleep. With him downstairs, I had no idea what other crazy idea he would get in his head and attack me over.

I cursed myself for even entertaining the idea that he had been transformed. He might have emerged from prison a changed man – but it was into someone even more controlling and unhinged.

Now that he was back he couldn't wait to act out all the sick fantasies he had been hoarding since being locked up. His clawing, crazed desire for me was suffocating. He had literally been counting the minutes we'd been apart, mourning the time we'd lost and vowing revenge on those he deemed to have been responsible for putting him away. I was permanently tense and rigid with fear, praying his lust would be sated quickly and his demands for sex would become less frequent. It was a forlorn hope. He had left prison like a demented animal, determined to celebrate his newfound freedom, unleashing all the sexual tension that had been building for three months.

His paranoia was now off the scale too. A few days after his release, I had barely walked in the door after visiting my parents when he pounced on me.

'Stand there,' he said, moving me to the middle of the living room.

'What is it?'

'Be quiet.' He pushed my hands down by my sides and walked around me, sniffing the air like a dog trying to detect a particular scent.

'What are you doing?' I said, trembling, racking my brains to think of anything I might have done to arouse his suspicion. Had I used a different shampoo, a strange soap? Had my dad been wearing a different aftershave, my mum a new perfume? Even though I had done nothing wrong, I felt guilty as sin.

'I said be quiet.' He stuck his nose into my hair and inhaled deeply. Then he was around my neck, my top, moving all over my body, sniffing frantically.

'Who have you been with?'

'No one.' I was now rigid with fear.

'Don't lie. I can tell. You don't smell like you. I can smell someone else. Who have you been kissing? Who have you been sleeping with?'

I had only been at my mum's for a matter of minutes. I hadn't even been away long enough to meet another man, let alone sleep with one. It was a ridiculous suggestion. I wondered where he had got the idea that I'd been unfaithful from. I still suspected his creepy relative James. I thought back to that time he'd come round to the cottage when ST wasn't here and tried it on with me. James gave the impression that ST told him everything that went on between us. It was hard for me to know if that was the case or whether he was just trying to make me feel uncomfortable.

'I've only been at my mum's,' I protested. 'Honest. I wouldn't go with anyone else.'

'You better not have,' he said, still sniffing me manically. 'It would kill me if that happened. Do you understand? It would absolutely kill me. I couldn't live with the thought of you being with anyone else. I love you so much. I would kill for you. Do you get that? Do you know how much I love you?'

I could only stand there, nodding, praying he was just trying to catch me out and not seriously thinking I'd been with anyone.

He launched into another of his 'togetherness' mantras. Being separated had made him even more of a zealot. And now that he was back, he renewed his desire to move away from Aberdare.

I might have got my way when I found our cottage, but it was only supposed to be a temporary move. He liked the idea of moving to somewhere where the nearest shop was a 15-minute drive away. He hated me going to visit my parents, even though my visits were becoming less and less frequent because he got so angry every time we weren't together. It just wasn't worth it.

He kept going on about finding a place near Brecon. I wasn't sure why he was so fixated on there. As far as I was aware he didn't have any connection with the place.

He just seemed to like it for its remoteness. He searched for the perfect place online and we went out there to view a number of different houses. Mercifully, they were all too near the town for his liking. For the time being we would be staying put, but I knew it was only a matter of time before he found a place he liked – and then God knows what would happen to me.

In the meantime he continued to control every aspect of my life – from the clothes I wore to my trips to the toilet. It didn't matter how many times he did it, I would never get used to him urinating between my legs while I sat on the toilet. The quiet solitude I had enjoyed while he was in prison was a fleeting memory. He had returned even more of a sex maniac, even more paranoid and controlling. He would have controlled each breath going in and out of my body if he could. I felt continually debased by him, like I wasn't human anymore.

I had to ask permission to leave the house. Mostly, he said no or demanded that he come too. There were times when, if I said I just wanted to pick something up from a particular shop, he appeared to say yes, but when I tried to leave I'd find that the door was locked and he'd pretend not to know where the key was. I had no option but to stay inside until he miraculously found the key, and by then it was too late to get to the shop.

One day I asked if I could pop round to see my

parents. My dad was still very ill with his heart problems and ST knew I had to check how he was.

'Okay, but only for 20 minutes,' he said. 'And I'll start the stopwatch so I'll know if you've been away for longer.'

I prepared to leave, but just as I was heading for the door he came bounding up to me.

'Take this.' He handed me a camera.

'What's that for?'

'I want you to document your every movement.'

I couldn't believe it.

'Look,' he said, showing me the display. 'It has a clock at the bottom to tell you what time the photograph was taken. When you go to your parents, take a photo to record every moment you are there, and I'll be able to tell by the time so there will be no missing minutes.'

It was insane, but I had no choice but to do as he said. With a heavy heart I trudged round the corner to my parents' house, snapping away so he couldn't accuse me of taking a detour. Once inside their house I tried to take the photographs discreetly because there was no way I could tell my mum and dad why I was taking so many pictures. Eventually, my mum did quiz me about what I was doing.

'It's a new camera but it's been playing up,' I said, hoping she'd buy my explanation and not probe further. 'I just want to check it's working okay. I'll delete them all later.'

When I saw the time and suddenly realised I'd been away for 18 minutes I said, 'I'd better go. He is cooking dinner,' and dashed out of the house. I scurried back to the cottage, hoping I'd made it back before the 20 minutes were up. As soon as I was in the door he snatched the camera off me and began scrolling through, checking the images and the time stamp.

'Here,' he said. 'What were you doing then?'

I looked at the screen. There were two minutes not accounted for between images.

'Where were you?' he asked.

'At my mum's,' I said, trying to stop my voice sounding too hysterical. 'We were just chatting. I didn't move from there.'

It was exhausting.

The rules didn't apply to him, of course. He could go out when he pleased. When he left I'd try the door. More often than not it would be locked, the key nowhere to be found. When he came back I'd ask why he locked me in.

'Did I? Sorry, it was an accident.'

When I told him I only wanted to get out to go to the shops for essential groceries he erupted.

'You're not taking this seriously!' he screamed. 'You don't understand how important this is.'

He sat me down and once more launched into his lecture on 'togetherness'. 'Together, together, together.'

I heard that word so many times it echoed endlessly around my head.

'Nothing can come between us, Sophie. I mean NOTHING! Every moment we are apart is like a knife through my heart. It kills me. Do you understand?'

I nodded weakly.

'You are torturing me,' he said, without irony. 'You are killing me. I can't live with you because I can't stand the seconds we are apart, and I can't live without you because not having you by my side makes life not worth living.'

'I'm sorry,' I whispered. What else could I say? I was sorry – that I'd somehow found myself living with an unhinged monster.

'The only solution is to die together,' he went on, his eyes red, his breath foul. He pulled me tighter and tighter to him. 'That's what I really want. I want us to die together. If I died, my soul would be devastated to know you were with someone else. And if you died, I couldn't go on, so the only solution is for us to die together.

'You would like that too, Sophie, wouldn't you? Tell me you want us to die together.'

'Yes, that's what I want.' Part of me knew just to say anything to satisfy him, but another part of me meant it. My spirit was completely crushed. It was March 2012. I had known him for less than two years but it seemed like a lifetime. I couldn't remember a time when he wasn't controlling me, wasn't ramming himself into me or forcing me down on him, wasn't screaming in my face or lecturing me on 'togetherness'.

Finally, he calmed down and wanted to go to bed. Sex – his version of it – was the only thing that stopped his lectures. That night it was particularly crazed. I was sure he was going to kill me. Maybe that was what he had meant with his rant earlier. This was it.

He forced my legs so wide I was sure they would snap. He drove my head so far into the pillow from behind that I nearly suffocated. Then he twisted me around and choked me until I had no breath left.

Then it was over. He was spent. I was gasping for life.

I lay there afterwards shivering, praying for salvation. In the darkness later I contemplated my lot. I was 19 years old and it felt like my life was a repeating loop of misery.

There was nothing, surely, that could make it worse.

That was until the morning when I woke, naked as usual, at seven. I was going through my daily itinerary of injuries and pain when he got up, stretched and, calmly turning to me, said, 'Today's the day we die.'

Without another word he walked calmly downstairs.

In that moment lots of thoughts go through your mind. How serious is he? Should I jump out of the window? Should I try to use the element of surprise and tackle him with whatever he returns with?

Mostly, however, you are just struck dumb, frantically trying to keep calm and think clearly.

When he returned with the Rambo knife he'd used to threaten me with in the lane I knew he was deadly serious. His eyes were like a shark's, devoid of emotion, red-raw from too much cannabis.

Suddenly, I felt a hundred times more vulnerable: still naked, trapped in a tiny room, my attacker standing between me and the only feasible escape route. Thinking his intention was to come for me, I braced myself. I was not remotely prepared for what he did next.

He clutched his genitals with one hand and put the blade to his penis. 'I'm not big enough for you, am I?' he said.

It was deranged. I couldn't believe what I was seeing – but I also couldn't stand back and watch him mutilate himself.

I tried to reason with him: 'What are you doing? This is crazy. Put it away now.'

'You do this to me.' He pushed the blade into his skin. 'It's YOUR fault.'

I jumped forward and grabbed the blade, slicing my hand. Before I knew what was happening he had pushed me onto the bed and was on top of me, the blade at my throat. How it hadn't already cut through my neck I'll never know.

When faced with extreme stress the body can respond in three ways – fight, flight or freeze. To fight him would have been suicide. He would have killed me for sure. I couldn't flee, and lying frozen with panic would not have helped. I'm not sure how I managed it, but in a moment of clarity I chose none of those options. Instead, I softly but surely began to stroke him, as though this was the sexiest foreplay imaginable.

It worked. He responded. He let go of the knife and, while he was preoccupied with satisfying himself, I kicked it from the bed. I thought the immediate danger had passed, but the situation was still precarious. Once he was done I tried to wriggle free of his clutches, but he grabbed me and put me in a headlock. We struggled and both fell off the bed, sending it across the floor on its wheels. He still had my head in a tight lock.

'Please,' I managed to say. 'I'll do anything, please, just leave me alone.'

He took me downstairs, ranting and raving about sick sexual fantasies. He kept saying how he wished he'd known me as a child, adding, 'I would have totally fucked you.'

It was beyond sick. If this was to be my final day on Earth I did not want to spend it listening to his perverted ramblings. I tried to remain calm, because if I'd shown any emotion it would have made it worse, but I couldn't control my shaking. My brain went a little bit dead. I felt numb, like I was not part of my body.

I was racking my brains, frantically trying to figure

how to get out, when there was a knock at the door. I was surprised he answered it.

The relief at seeing my mum there quickly turned to horror, as I feared he might drag her into this nightmare. As soon as she saw my face she knew something had happened. She tried to grab me through the gap in the door but he was too strong. He blocked her and pulled me back inside. When she disappeared, shouting that she was going to get my dad and sister, I prayed she was going to be back soon.

He tried to drag me upstairs. Once again I had a moment of clarity. I knew that if I went upstairs I would never come down again. 'I need the toilet,' I said, knowing full well that he'd follow me in. I had to slow him down, give Mum time to get to the house and back again.

They were back even quicker than I'd hoped. My mum, my sister and my dad, bless him. What an effort that would have been. He must have known I was in real danger.

He couldn't do anything in front of them. Not even he would have dared do that. He was already trying to play down the seriousness to them. It was only when he joined me in the bedroom, as I chucked on the first clothes I could find, that the mask slipped once more. His voice was perfectly calm as he spoke the words that would haunt me forever: 'I could break your neck now and no one would know.'

I didn't hang around to test that theory. I jumped back down the stairs two at a time and ran out of the house, past my waiting family and up to their house. I collapsed on the door and my father had to carry me in. Once inside, I became hysterical. All the stress was catching up with me, the adrenalin was wearing off, and in its place came the realisation of how close I'd come to death.

I wasn't making sense. Mum guided me up to my room so it was just the two of us and I wouldn't feel overcrowded or overwhelmed. I was exhausted, completely spent. All I wanted to do was sleep. I couldn't even begin to tell my parents what had just happened. I couldn't even believe it myself.

I crashed out for several hours, and even when I woke I still felt like I was dreaming. The world seemed a confusing and distorted place.

My mum stayed by my side. She pleaded with me not to go back to him. While I had been sleeping they'd called the police. My mum revealed that she had been talking to the police for months about how concerned she was for my safety. I had no idea.

The moment I heard the police were involved I panicked. He had conditioned me to fear them. I was terrified that he would know if I talked to them. How could I begin to tell them what I'd been through? They couldn't protect me from him. He would kill me for sure. I thought of him standing outside our house in the middle of the night with the petrol canister. His threats against my dad. We were all in danger if I cooperated. There was no way I could do that.

My parents and sister despaired of me. 'Tell the police everything,' they said. 'They are here to help you.'

I just shook my head and shut down. It was all too much.

Based on my mum's complaint, police officers went to the cottage and spoke to him. I could imagine what he was like, calm and charming. Once she'd seen the state of my hand I had to tell her about the knife. They took the blade to test for my DNA. They detained him and explained to us that he would go to a psychiatric hospital for assessment.

This is the end, my family said. Surely you see now what he is like – how dangerous he is. Why would you go back into that house?

They would never understand.

I couldn't leave him.

I was under his control.

He had threatened to burn my family's house down.

He would kill us all.

I was terrified of him.

There was nothing else I could do.

I had to go back.

Chapter 17

I slumped into the taxi. It was like my mind was not my own. The driver tried to engage me in conversation but I just stared out of the window, barely registering him or the world outside. There could have been a building on fire or a five-car pile-up on the other side of the road and I wouldn't have noticed.

It was a 15-minute drive to Merthyr Tydfil. The taxi driver came to a halt outside an imposing grey building. I paid the fare and trudged towards the front door of St Tydfil's Hospital.

For my parents, this had been especially hard. They must have been reminded of the early days, when I wouldn't listen to their appeals. Here I was, two years on, going to see the man who had attacked me with a knife, who'd threatened to kill me – and them – and who was being detained in a psychiatric hospital for assessment.

They knew he was dangerous, but they didn't know how dangerous. I still hadn't told them the extent of what I had been through, yet they were still trying to convince me to see sense. They couldn't understand. And how could they, when I couldn't even comprehend what I was doing? I couldn't explain what was going on in my head. He had utter control over me, and even when he wasn't there physically he still pulled the strings.

I was slipping into a hole deeper than I'd ever been in before. I thought I knew about depression after the experiences of my early teens, but it was nothing compared to this. I already had complex post-traumatic stress disorder following the car accident with Dad and the one with ST, and having a knife put against my throat had pushed me to the edge of sanity. I was utterly confused. I didn't know what to do. The only thing I knew was how scared of him I was. And the only remedy was to do exactly what he said.

So when he phoned me from the psychiatric hospital and told me to visit him that is what I did.

When the police first told me he was being detained I felt elation. I prayed that they would keep him in for good. They said it would take two weeks at least. But I knew. I knew it would only be a matter of time. Being in prison hadn't stopped him, so I doubted being in a hospital would.

Within a day or so he was phoning and texting. 'Come

and visit me now.' No apology. No explanation. No attempt to get me to understand why he had decided to end our lives and come at me with a knife.

As soon as I walked into his ward I knew he wouldn't be in for long. His demeanour was sunny and smiley. He bounded up to greet me. I saw a nurse and a doctor smile as though they were witnessing love's young dream in the flesh. Did they not know what he was in there for? It was like watching a consummate actor at work. He could turn the charm on like a tap.

'What a nice man,' one of the nurses said. It was sickening to watch. He had them eating out of his palm.

And then, as soon as we were alone, the act stopped. He demanded the phone card and cigarettes he'd ordered me to bring him. Then the eyes darkened, the voice deepened.

'Who have you been screwing, then, while I've been away?' he said, gripping my shoulders so tightly, staring into my eyes for signs that might betray me.

'You know I haven't.'

'It's your fault I am in here,' he said. 'You drive me to do these things. You know how much I love you and can't bear being apart from you.'

He was trying to make me feel bad for his behaviour: threatening me with a knife and vowing to break my neck. I could scarcely believe it, but I'd heard it so many times I had no response.

'Why are you acting like that?' I said, pointing out to the ward where the doctors were.

'Because I want to get out. I'm playing their game.'

He started kissing me. I tried to wriggle free.

'Not in here,' I said.

'Come with me, then.' He pulled me towards the toilet.

'No,' I said, standing firm. 'I don't want to.'

He pulled me and I nearly fell into him. He hauled open the door, bundled me inside and locked it. He undid my clothes and took down his trousers. I thought of the smiling nurse just yards away. If only they saw this side of him. I tried to fend him off but it was no use. He made me have sex right there in the hospital toilet.

When it came time to leave I walked back into the ward burning with shame, feeling everyone's eyes on me as if they knew. I hadn't even made it home before the text messages started, demanding I return the following day. It was his right. He expected nothing less. I tried to explain that it would be difficult, and he launched into a tirade of abuse. 'Do you not love me?' 'Is it because you're sleeping with someone else?'

And so, to my parents' dismay, back I went every day for hours at a time. The more I went, the bolder he became. We were sitting in the communal living area when he began pawing at me. His hands were groping me all over.

'Hey!' a nurse shouted. 'Cool it. None of that in here.'

'Sorry,' he said, practically fluttering his eyelids at her. 'I can't help it. I just get carried away. I love her so much.'

He must have thought his mission to be released was accomplished, because a few days after that he got careless. Normally, he waited until we were alone before starting on me, but this time he didn't seem to care who was listening.

'Everything is your fault,' he said. He was now turning really nasty. 'You got me in here and you won't help get me out.'

'What was I supposed to do?' I said, genuinely perplexed.

'You could have slept with the judge,' he said, in all seriousness. 'You could have fucked him in return for letting me off.'

Even for him, this was crazy. What judge? Like that scenario would ever happen. He lived in a sick fantasy world.

'You shut up!' The sister on duty had clearly overheard him and came over to tick him off.

He did his usual charm act, but no sooner had she gone than he launched into another tirade.

'Right, that's it,' the sister said. She hadn't gone. She was still listening in. 'Visit over.'

He tried to protest but she was adamant: I was to go immediately.

I hoped these little incidents might convince them what a nasty piece of work he really was. After three weeks of assessments he had to go before a mental-health tribunal, which would determine whether he was a risk to himself, me or the public. They ruled that he was not. On the one hand I couldn't believe it, yet on the other, had I really expected anything else? He had managed to do exactly what I had feared – pull the wool over everyone's eyes.

Why could they not see what an evil manipulator he was? How could they not tell he was lying and playing along when he answered their questions? Did attacking me with a knife and threatening to castrate himself not count for anything?

It seemed not.

I was on my own. If the authorities didn't believe there was anything wrong with him, maybe it was all in my head and I was the one who was wrong.

Maybe he was right. Was it all my fault?

I had been staying at my mum's while he was being assessed, but now that he was being released I had to go back to the cottage. He still had power of attorney over my money, and without access to my benefits I was broke. I even had to ask my parents for money to buy toilet roll. My parents tried to stop me but I was completely at his mercy.

It was with great trepidation that I walked back into

the cottage, in preparation for his return. It was strange setting foot back in there. It looked the same – dark and imposing – but there was a weird energy, as though in the air hung remnants of my struggle for survival and my frantic escape. The atmosphere felt heavy and oppressive.

I walked upstairs to the bedroom. The bed clothes were still in a mess, the bed itself sitting at an angle from being knocked across the room. This must be what forensic detectives feel like when they enter the scene of a crime. The telltale signs of the skirmish could be felt in every corner.

The stillness unnerved me. It was hardly ever quiet in that house. There was always noise – usually his ranting, or music blaring or the disturbing soundtracks to his sick videos. To be here in the silence, knowing what was coming back, was no comfort at all.

Throughout his time in hospital I'd wondered whether he suspected I was speaking to the police, and if, on his release, he would return and kill me. I would soon find out.

I sat down and waited for the storm to come.

It duly arrived when he came crashing through the door. He had only one thing on his mind. That was another trick he had managed to pull off in the hospital – convincing them he was not a sex maniac. No one had to convince me, though. I knew it well enough.

It was as though nothing had changed, or, at the very most, someone had only briefly pressed pause on the madness. He was as crazed as ever. He wanted to get stoned, have sex, play his computer games and be bathed in UV light. He wanted to control every aspect of my life.

I assumed my role – the ragdoll to which he could do as he pleased.

I had been living back in the cottage for only a week or so when a man and a woman came to the door. Luckily, I answered the door, as he was engrossed in a computer game.

They introduced themselves as a psychiatrist and a mental-health nurse. I thought, *They must be here to check up on him.* They weren't. They were here for me. The police had sent them. They handed me an envelope in which they said was a document known as an Osman letter. Such a letter, they said, is issued when the police have intelligence that there is a high risk to someone's life but they don't have enough evidence to arrest the potential killer.

They asked if I was aware that I was in grave danger. I was struck dumb. I couldn't believe this was happening – not the fact that the police thought I was at risk of being murdered, but that these people had come to my door about it. They warned me to move out of the house.

I took the letter from them and ushered them away.

He shouted through, asking who was at the door. I made up some story about missing a hospital appointment. Thankfully, he bought it and didn't probe further. When I had a moment I looked at the letter.

At the top it read: 'The police are in possession of information which suggests that there is a risk of a threat to your life.'

It described his mental health as having worsened considerably to the point where he'd developed extreme jealousy and paranoia and delusional thoughts in prison.

I read the words, but instead of fear I felt anger.

The letter had been prompted by my mum's conversations with the police. The medical professionals should have gone to my parents' house. Instead, they came to the cottage. My God, if I hadn't lied through my teeth about who was at the door … If he had found out who they were and why they were here, he would have gone berserk. And if he found out that such a letter even existed and that it originated from the police then I would be dead. I couldn't believe they'd turned up at the house. Were they for real? Did they not realise how dangerous that was? Do they even think of these things?

They feared I was about to be murdered yet turned up in such a cack-handed fashion that could have guaranteed it actually happened. You could not make it up.

And why did no one get it? I could never leave him. Getting a warning in a letter wasn't going to change anything.

No one could help. There was no way out. I just had to find a way to survive – by any means possible.

Chapter 18

It was an unlikely companion, but in that house of horrors a little white Furby baby was one of my few possessions and sometimes felt like the only friend I had. I had found the vintage furry toy on eBay, not long after we moved in, when I still had some of my own money. I'd always wanted one when I was younger and finally I could have one. I loved its funny little face, the pink ears and the fact that it gurgled cutely and spoke in a strange little voice whenever it was cuddled or played with.

That hadn't happened for a long time. For months it had just sat on a shelf downstairs, staring out. I often looked at it and wondered about the other houses it might have lived in. I imagined its previous owner might have been a little girl who played with it religiously, showering it with love. It would have played its part in a happy childhood, full of innocence and wonder.

And then it arrived in this house. What terrors had it witnessed? If only it could speak now. What stories would it tell? I wasn't even sure if the batteries still worked. Its cute gurgling was not the sort of sound that was welcome in this place.

These were some of the things I wondered about when I was forced to sit down, on his lap, where he hugged me, not in the way a young child might cuddle a favourite toy, but squeezing me so tight until I could hear my back crack. Only then would he let me go.

It was July 2012 and it was now over two years since my life had been taken over. I had been as innocent as a young girl before fate delivered me to this monster. Now I was corrupted and broken, innocence lost forever.

That little Furby was a last reminder of a time when I was still able to cherish the fun things in life. Now all I craved was normality – a meal I could choose for myself, a minute alone in the toilet, a night's rest not punctuated by the demands of a sex-crazed beast.

Since the knife attack he had been growing increasingly volatile. We rarely went out, but when we did he was no longer able to control his violent temper. We were walking in Aberdare Park when he started shouting and bawling. I can't even remember what I had done to enrage him.

'You're crazy,' I said to him and tried to walk away. 'I can't do this anymore.'

He grabbed me by my jacket and picked me up by it, lifting my feet off the ground. He shook me so much my head hurt.

'Listen,' he growled. 'If you leave, I'll tell your dad exactly what you're like – everything you've done and what you're into.'

I froze. Dad was still extremely unwell. I feared any more stress like the type he'd endured over the knife incident might tip him over the edge.

'I won't leave you,' I whimpered, as he put me down.

Not long after that we were walking in Aberdare town. There were lots of shoppers, as it was a nice sunny summer day. A man happened to walk past. I had no idea who he was but he smiled at me as he passed.

Bang! The next thing I knew, a water bottle had been bashed over my head.

'Bitch!' he screamed. 'Have you done him as well?'

I nursed my head but tried to placate him, as there were so many people around. It was mortifying and terrifying at the same time.

A similar thing happened when we took some clothes to the charity shop. Something completely innocuous sparked his fury. He threw the clothes all over the road. I walked away from him but he started following me, shouting obscenities at the top of his lungs: 'Slut! Slag! Bitch!'

Everyone around was looking. My face burned with embarrassment. He caught up with me, grabbed me by my coat and slapped me across the face. I felt the tears well up. I just wanted to die. He dragged me back to the cottage, where he continued to rant and rave for an hour. When he was done, he expected me to tolerate being in bed with him. He took it as his right.

Often, he slapped my backside hard during sex, but when that wasn't enough for him he reached for my hair brush. He whacked me so hard it broke in two.

If the physical violence wasn't torture enough, I had to endure his taunts as well. He brought up the time we visited the Giant's Tooth viewpoint and he forced sex on me from behind after pushing me to the ground. Seeing how much even the mention of it made me squirm, he leered, 'That was one of the best shags I've ever had.'

Watching his disgusting porn films must have constantly given him ideas, because he then came out with something he wanted to try – me urinating on him during sex.

I suffered it all in silence. He went down to get a cup of tea while I lay there hating a world that allowed monsters like him to live while innocent victims of crime lost their lives every day. He returned, put the cup of tea by the bed and tried to instigate sex again.

'I hate you,' I said. The words came out before I thought of the consequences.

He kicked me out of bed with such force that I didn't touch the side on the way to the floor. He grabbed the mug and threw the tea in my face. I screamed in shock. He jumped out of bed and started kicking me in the stomach. My face was burning and my eyes were stinging. He then left the bedroom. I got up and tried to go downstairs but he kept chasing me back up, and in the end he held the door shut, keeping me in there for hours and only letting me out when I begged him to open the door.

After that incident he decreed that I could only venture out to see my family – under strict rules, to a set timescale and only if I produced documentary evidence of my visit and accounted for every second.

It was the only freedom I had, so I had to grab it when the chance arose. When he relaxed his grip of me and turned his attention to something else, it was usually my cue to try to slip out for 20 minutes. That was what I was thinking one afternoon when I reached for my shoes and started to put them on.

Suddenly, he ripped them from my grasp and threw them against the wall.

'Running away, are you?' he said. 'I don't think so.'

He picked me up, pushed me onto the sofa and pinned me down.

'You're not leaving,' he spat.

For a moment he stood over me, pushing me back into the upholstery. *Where is this going?* I wondered. *What has triggered this?*

'I'm just going to Mum and Dad's,' I whimpered.

'Not today.' He pushed himself off and flew around the downstairs rooms, locking the door and windows. He picked up my shoes and took them off somewhere, to hide them, I assumed.

'What are you doing?' I said, my voice breaking. The air crackled with menace. This wasn't good. I sat up.

'Don't move!' he shouted.

What crazed thoughts were in his mind? What delusions? I tried to think of anything that might have upset him. I hardly left the house. There was nothing, surely, that could have inspired such fury.

'I don't want you leaving here,' he said. 'You are not leaving here. You don't understand. We have to be together.'

I tried to placate him, hoping my soothing voice would calm him down.

'I do understand,' I said.

'You don't. You don't get it. If you did, you wouldn't try to leave. If we were apart for just 5 minutes every day over 50 years that would mean 63 days apart. That's over two months we would lose. Is that what you want?'

I had no idea if what he was saying was accurate. Given the amount of time he devoted to this 'togetherness' obsession I suspected it was true, but who examined time like that?

Where was he going with this? What was he trying to achieve? I'd heard his lectures before. I'd endured his obsessive, controlling behaviour. But this was something else. He was building to something.

He made me sit on the sofa while he ranted. Minutes turned into an hour. Then it was two.

'Please,' I said. 'I really need to go to the bathroom.'

'I'll take you.'

It didn't matter how many times he accompanied me to the toilet, I would never find it acceptable. I detested it when he urinated between my legs. It was degrading and as dehumanising as what he did next – carry me upstairs to have sex.

When he was done I tried to slip away. It had been hours since I'd tried to go to my mum's house and I felt suffocated. I thought he was sleeping but he grabbed me.

'No, you're staying here,' he said.

'I just want to get up.'

'We'll go downstairs when I say.'

Another hour passed and then he took me down and put me back on the sofa.

'I'm hungry. When are we getting something to eat?' I said.

'You're not eating,' he said. 'You are just going to sit here and not move.'

I tried to protest but he slammed me back into the sofa. He went into the kitchen. I expected him to return and start feeding me, but he just made himself something and brought nothing for me.

'Can I get something to eat, please?'

He ignored me and sat back down beside me, pulling me onto his lap again. I just had to remain calm. This could have been a passing mood, but something about the tone in his voice and his demeanour suggested it was different. He was completely serious.

On and on he went about 'togetherness': 'We will be together forever. We will never be parted. Always together.'

'We are together,' I stressed. 'We will be together forever. You don't have to worry.'

'You don't understand,' he kept saying. He got up and started pacing the room. If I moved, he screamed in my face, 'Stay there!'

Hours passed and still I could not move. He refused to let me eat or drink. I felt nauseous. He was still pacing the floor, lecturing me on 'togetherness'.

'Together, together, together.'

I was zoning out, but I jolted back to reality at the sight of a huge spider scurrying across the floor. I've had a phobia of creepy-crawlies ever since I was young, but spiders hold a particular fear. I let out a scream and tucked my legs under me on the sofa. He turned and spotted what was causing me alarm. He knew all about my phobia. He picked up the spider and threw it at my face. I screamed and jumped up and down, shaking and rubbing myself down manically. I could feel it everywhere.

He laughed.

'Where is it, where is it?' I said. Half of my problem is not knowing where it is once I've seen a spider in the room.

'Up your top,' he said.

I screamed again and shook myself once more.

'You know I'm scared of spiders,' I protested, but he didn't care. He was enjoying watching me squirm.

He jumped back on the sofa and pinned me down.

'Stop it, you're suffocating me,' I said. He was smothering my face, pulling my head into his chest. Another fear I have is of enclosed spaces. He knew all about my claustrophobia. It took on many forms. I didn't like lifts or changing rooms in shops or the feeling of being in a car with the doors locked. He swung his legs over me and held me so tightly that I thought he was going to crush me to death. I started panicking, gasping for breath and trying to free my arms. He increased the pressure.

'Stop! You're going to kill me.'

He released his grip and I clambered up the back of the sofa, gasping for breath.

'You're sick,' I said.

'You're pathetic. Imagine being scared of a little spider.'

He got a kick out of seeing me scared. It was actually turning him on. I knew what that meant. He wrestled with me again but it was pointless to resist. He grabbed me and hauled me upstairs. He was even more frenzied than usual, throwing me around and pushing my legs apart. I tried to switch off.

Nothing lasts forever, I said to myself. *Nothing. Everything comes to an end. Nothing lasts forever. This will be over soon.*

Over and over I repeated this mantra to myself, trying to take my mind off the brutality.

'Move!' he shouted, manoeuvring me to another position, something he had no doubt seen in one of his hardcore porn films. 'Not like that. Come on, put some effort in.'

I had to do as I was told or the agony would only be prolonged. As much as it pained me, the goal was to bring him to a climax as quickly as possible so it was over and done with. No sooner had he done so than he took me back downstairs. If there was a point he was trying to make, he hadn't done it yet.

I was losing track of time. How many hours had passed since he'd stopped me from leaving? It was long past midnight, of that I was sure. At this time of year it didn't stay dark outside for long. Not that we saw much daylight. With the curtains drawn it was impossible to tell what was happening. I looked for the telltale signs of light around the windows. It looked like dawn was breaking.

'Are you going to let me eat something?' I said.

He shook his head. 'You'll eat when I say.'

'Please,' I begged. 'I'm starving.'

He cast a withering eye over my body. 'And you could do with losing some more weight. You got fat while I was away.'

My legs started to cramp from sitting on the sofa for so long. I tried to stretch them, but I needed to move around to get the feeling back.

'Can I stretch my legs?' I asked.

'You're not going anywhere.' He sat down next to me and pulled me onto his lap again. My legs ached at the sudden movement. 'There you go,' he said, as though he'd soothed them.

Sitting there, hunched up in pain and mental anguish, I thought about my parents begging me not to come back to this house. I thought about the Osman letter. My mum and the police were trying to protect me, but I had come back to this madman. I didn't think I had a choice. If I hadn't returned then he could have killed me or them, or all of us. Now I realised that coming back wasn't going to change that. It didn't matter what I did, I was going to pay with my life.

My skin started to prickle, my pulse quickened. The last time I'd felt this way was when he'd entered the bedroom with the knife. I could feel conflicting impulses: to fight my way out; to try to escape by whatever means possible; or to freeze like a rabbit in the headlights and await my fate. Fight, flight or freeze. I had been in this situation before. I knew what I had to do: stay calm, keep my wits about me; try to reason with him; do nothing to antagonise or inflame this powder-keg situation.

How could I keep a clear head, though? Hunger pangs knotted my stomach, my limbs ached, I was being suffocated by this brute and I was still twitchy with the thought of a spider climbing all over the sofa. I had to hope it had sensed the danger and scurried off somewhere to hide. Part of me envied it. Its chances of survival ranked higher than mine right now.

'You are my baby,' he kept saying. 'We are destined to be together forever. We are like Romeo and Juliet. We will die together. Together for eternity.'

I tried to prepare for anything. What would he do? Strangle me? Had he bought another knife? Was his goal to starve me to death?

I thought of my family. How long would they go without hearing from me before they came to investigate? Would the police follow up their letter to check I was still alive? How long did I have? Hours? Days? Would they come when it was too late?

Morning came and went, and still we sat there. He was drifting in and out of sleep, but he was holding me so tight that any time I tried to wriggle free he woke and pulled me closer to him.

By midday he rallied and again fixed himself something to eat, while I continued to starve. It was torture watching him while my stomach contracted and my throat gasped for water. Refuelled, his sex drive returned. He stood up and, holding my hand, led me upstairs. As I took each step, I repeated my mantra: *Nothing lasts forever. Everything comes to an end. Nothing lasts forever.*

I continued saying it throughout the ordeal that followed. Each time his hands went to my throat I tensed. Was this the moment? Was he going to throttle me one final time? I was so scared, my whole body was shaking. I couldn't control it.

'You're having an orgasm,' he said, looking sickeningly proud of himself.

No, I wanted to scream, *I am in mortal fear for my life – this is not a sexual response.* I tried desperately to control it. There were moments when I felt I would faint from the strain, but somehow I kept it together until it was finally over.

Remaining calm took all my strength. I tried to hide my fear and make out that this was normal behaviour.

'Can we go outside?' I said, after another couple of

hours had passed and he refused to move. 'Get some fresh air. Together.'

'We are not going anywhere,' he said. His voice was slurring. The lack of sleep and proper daylight were affecting him too. But he would not be deflected from whatever his plan was. I wanted to wash. I felt disgusting, and I thought I might be able to drink some of the water splashed on my face.

'You want to go to the bathroom?' he asked.

I nodded.

'Okay, then, let's go.' He picked me up and carried me to the bathroom. Instead of letting me wash, though, he pushed me over the bath and forced himself on me. My whole body felt like it was crying out in pain. It would be better if he did kill me, I thought, at least then this torture would be over. He dragged me to the living room, to the sofa, onto his lap. I couldn't bear him touching me. His very being repulsed me. He kept ranting but it was becoming incoherent, or was it that I was struggling to focus?

'Can I at least sit on the floor?' I mumbled.

'No,' he grunted, pulling me closer on his lap. 'We were meant to be together. You are my baby.'

Together, together, together. That word echoed around my brain. We couldn't be more together. Together. Yes, together. We needed to be together. I started to believe the things he was saying. I must have been losing my mind.

I was aware of the rain falling outside. It was night time again. We had been like this for nearly 36 hours straight. Or was it longer? I had no idea. No food. No sleep. Just sitting on the sofa, our only breaks when he led me upstairs.

This wasn't a life. It was a living hell. How long could I last like this? I had no idea, but I knew it wasn't long. I didn't have a strong constitution as it was, and I imagined my organs failing and my body slowly decaying.

I had to find a way out of this. Surely he would tire and crash out? On and on he droned, though. Together, together. Was he trying to break whatever was left of my spirit? If so, he was succeeding.

It became increasingly hard to think straight.

There were more trips upstairs. I'd lost track of the hours in between. I was struggling even to remember my mantras. *Nothing lasts, nothing lasts.*

I started to doubt them. Maybe this would last forever. Maybe there was no escape.

He was becoming more frenzied, goading me after forcing himself on me again with, 'What's it like being raped in your own bed?'

I knew only too well.

When we went back downstairs it was daylight again. Day two, was it, or had it been longer?

'Please, let me have something to eat,' I whimpered. 'I am dying.'

He smiled and nodded. He raved incoherently. He was going to kill me. He'd kill himself. He'd kill both of us. 'It's the way it has to be,' he said.

My mind was scrambled. I had to keep thinking straight. I had to stay alert so that when the moment came I would be ready. It was hard, though. I was bone-tired and light-headed. It felt like my brain was being starved of oxygen.

Time wore on. Day turned to night, and then into light once more. Still the rain fell. His trips upstairs became less frequent. He was tiring.

I was aware of a buzzing noise. It took me a while to place the sound. It was something familiar but in my semi-conscious state it was hard to pinpoint what it was. He got up and found the source. It was my phone. Someone was trying to contact me. I was missed. My mum and dad must be worried.

He put it down.

'Who is it?' I said.

'No one.'

'My mum?'

'No one. No one is coming to save you,' he said, sitting back down.

Was that true? Surely it wasn't. Surely someone would rescue me? There had to be someone out there who could hear my cries for help.

I started praying to God and the angels. *Help me,*

please. Deliver me from this evil. Show me a sign that you are listening. I need your help. Now is the time. He is going to kill me. Please, please help me.

The voice, when it came, startled me. It surprised us both. It took us a moment to register. It sounded like a ghost or some kind of sprite, chattering away.

It was the Furby! It had woken up and was gurgling away on the shelf.

'Bloody stupid toy,' he muttered, and he was up, snatching it from the shelf.

'Careful,' I said softly.

'How do you switch this thing off?' He was shaking it up and down. It only made it chuckle more. 'Bloody hell!' He moved towards the door in the kitchen. The Furby was going crazy.

I sat up. Had my prayers been answered?

My phone buzzed again. He grabbed it and was punching something into it, still heading for the door.

'What are you doing?' I called.

'Texting your mum,' he said. 'You won't be seeing them for a while.'

He had the phone in his hand. The Furby was still chattering away under his arm.

'And this is going in the bloody bin,' he said.

I heard him unlock the door. There was a rush of air from outside. I could hear the rain pelt off the patio.

I was on my feet, running towards the door. This was my chance. My one chance. I got to the door. He was out by the bin, still distracted by the phone. I had no shoes or socks on, but I slipped out of the door and ran. Into the lane, around the corner, running as fast as I could, the rain in my eyes, feet slipping on the slabs, stones stabbing my soles like knives. I don't know where the energy came from but it propelled me home. The last few yards seemed like miles, but I ate them up in lightning-quick time. I raced up the path to our door and banged on it with all the strength I had left.

'Let me in!'

The door opened. I caught a glimpse of the shocked expression on my mum's face as I barged past her and crumpled into a heap on the floor. I tried to speak but couldn't form a sentence. I was gulping huge lungfuls of air with each breath. But I didn't care. I was free. I was out of that house.

My prayers had been answered. I was home.

Chapter 19

I wanted to sleep for a hundred-thousand years. After making it home I immediately crashed out. I was utterly spent. I have no idea how long I did sleep, but it wasn't as deep as I'd hoped. It was fitful. I had terrible dreams and often woke up thinking I was back in the cottage. When I eventually woke properly I was very weak. I barely had the strength to cry, but the tears did come – in pitiful sobs. It was going to be a long road to recovery.

My mum told me I had been talking gibberish when I first got home. I couldn't string a sentence together. It was only through speaking to her that I realised he had kept me prisoner in that house without food or water or sleep for three days.

I wasn't entirely sure because I'd lost all sense of time in there. It had been such a struggle to keep it together. I was mentally exhausted as well as physically broken.

Everything went black and white. I cried for three days but then suddenly I stopped. I no longer cared whether I lived or died. It is a very strange feeling when you no longer care about anything. It's as if everything is in slow motion. You are not real, nothing is real, there is no colour, your mind has completely shut down and you are going on autopilot.

I felt like the living dead.

There wasn't a sense of elation at being free of him. The level of control he exerted wasn't something you could turn off like a switch. I felt mournful and utterly depressed.

While I'd been asleep my mum had phoned the police. Two male officers came to the house. Now I knew I had to cooperate with them. Before, I thought speaking to them would put lives in danger. Since ST had made it clear that he wanted to murder me regardless, I knew I had to take the risk.

That said, speaking to the police wasn't easy. I was still apprehensive and unsure about what it would all mean. It was so much to take in. Cooperating with the police would mean becoming a witness, hopefully leading to a prosecution and conviction. Would I be able to handle all of that? I was still shaking from my ordeal and fearful for my life. It didn't help that one of the officers was quite aggressive with me when I didn't answer as fully as he wanted.

'She has Asperger syndrome,' my mother explained. 'That means communication can be difficult. You have to be patient with her.'

They sent for two senior female officers, whose approach was instantly more sympathetic. I was too scared to come downstairs when they arrived, so they came up and suggested we speak in my sister's bedroom. They spoke softly and kindly, they didn't rush me, and I felt like they understood.

They told me he had been arrested and was being held on remand. In order to keep him off the streets they needed to know how dangerous he was. They explained that there was a facility in Merthyr Tydfil, the Sexual Assault Referral Centre (SARC) – the first of its kind in Wales, specifically providing help and support to victims of rape and sexual assault – where they wanted to conduct a proper interview. I would give a full statement about everything I'd been through over the past two years.

When I arrived there I could see that it was a safe environment, geared up for people who have suffered the same type of trauma as me. At first I was a little reticent about opening up. I felt shame and embarrassment at what he had done to me. However, once I started speaking I found it easier, and slowly I began to recount my ordeal. Revisiting the violent attacks and verbal abuse I had endured was tough, but I knew I had to tell the police to have a chance of getting him convicted.

The interview took hours. I was finally getting into my flow when the police suddenly stopped the interview because they said the centre was closing. I couldn't believe it. It had taken me this long to finally start speaking and now they were terminating the interview. They asked if I could go back but I didn't want to go back. They had broken the flow. Going there once was hard enough. I should have been allowed to keep going, however long it took. It was a mistake on the police's part. Once I returned home the memories of what I'd been talking about swirled around my mind. It was like I was reliving the horror. They wanted to arrange another interview but by then the thought scared me. I was too traumatised. What was the point of having a specialised centre if it didn't accommodate the specific needs of the victims and instead created a situation that made it harder for them to tell their stories? Surely the police could have asked for it to stay open? It was deeply frustrating. I felt that it was a huge missed opportunity. There were lots of things that I didn't get a chance to talk about.

At the same time that I was being interviewed, police went to the cottage and conducted a search of the property. They seized his laptop and even retrieved the Furby from the bin, where I'd said it would be.

Until my escape I had kept the full extent of what had happened from my parents. It was traumatic for them to hear what I had been through. It was difficult for them to comprehend that someone could be so evil. It was a lot for them to deal with – not just the extreme violence but the control he had over my life and finances. They knew more than anyone the struggles I'd had in my early years, and then for me to face this, just at the point when I was trying to engage more with the outside world, was incomprehensible for them.

'He controlled my every action, movement and feelings,' I told my parents. 'Everything revolved around him. He was like a god. I was so scared of him. He could be so violent. He tried to kill me. He used sex as a weapon to crush me down and rid me of my confidence.'

They sat in silence as I recounted some of what had happened, shaking their heads in disbelief. There was no point going into every detail.

'When you are full of bruises, bite marks and scratches, your clothes have been physically torn and you look in the mirror, you feel ashamed and embarrassed and also a sense of guilt, like it was somehow your fault that these things happened,' I said to them. 'He made me feel like it was my fault. If only I would be a "good girl". He would say to me, "What does it feel like to be raped in your own bed?"'

Speaking about it made it seem real. Like it was no longer something that existed only in my head. And that brought a fresh fear. For a long time I thought they would release him and he would come for me. I was scared for my life all over again. He would know I had been talking about him.

My parents found it difficult to understand at first, and for quite a few weeks everything was in limbo, as no one quite knew what to do. They were so shocked by what had happened and how I had kept quiet about it for so long. My parents blamed themselves, saying that they should have noticed something sooner.

'If you had known it just would have made things worse,' I said. 'It was better and safer for me that you didn't know.'

My brother took it especially hard. He had always known there was something wrong with ST. He had tried to stop me seeing him. When he heard the extent of what I'd been through it was hard for him to comprehend. He really struggled and tried to completely block it out by self-medicating by drinking too much. An abusive relationship doesn't just affect one person – it has far-reaching consequences.

I didn't know what to do with myself to begin with, having been under someone's control for two years and then suddenly having no one to tell me what to do. I had to learn how to do things again, like making my own decisions – even simple things like when to go to bed. Mentally, I was a baby, and I had to quickly become an adult again.

The longer ST spent in custody, however, the more I began to take back control of my life. At first I couldn't face going back into the cottage. It represented so much misery. I hated the thought that it was so close. But it was time to cut all ties with it – and him.

I'd also had ST's mum on the phone, demanding that his belongings be sent to her. I couldn't put it off any longer. I formally gave notice to end the tenancy. Even though the landlord knew that the reason for us leaving was his tenant getting arrested, and even though he'd detected my reticence before we signed the lease, he refused to give me back my deposit. He didn't give a reason. In the grand scheme of things £850 was nothing, but I had no money of my own and it would have been good to have it, as it was rightfully mine. Until I managed to get power of attorney over my benefits, I was going to be without any income.

I had to summon a lot of courage just to walk through the cottage door. I asked my mum to accompany me because I couldn't face going there alone. Once we got there, though, I asked if she could leave me to it. I wanted to do it alone.

When I stepped inside I shuddered. The place held a lot of dark energy. Images of Star cowering in pain and his cruelty flooded my brain. I couldn't help but recall the many times he had abused me, and seeing the mirror, with his lecture on 'togetherness', was a lasting reminder of the horror I'd endured.

I looked at the walls and remembered him scrawling obscene messages on there in invisible pen, which would only show up under UV light. The landlord or future tenant would get a shock if they ever saw it.

I wanted to take everything down, rip up all the photographs, take back the things he had bought with my money. I put his clothes in bin bags and just threw them downstairs for his mum to collect. I thought about setting fire to them. I wish I had.

I chucked most of the rest of the stuff into three bin bags – one for me, one for the dump and one to go to ST's mum. I found the letters he'd demanded I write while he was in prison. I couldn't bear to look at them and threw them in the bag with the rest of his things.

Finally, I locked up and returned the items to his mum. It wasn't long before she was on the phone to my mum.

'Where is his laptop?' she asked.

Mum told her that the police had confiscated it.

'And where are his bankcards?'

Mum said, 'Sophie cut them up, just as he did to hers.'

She wasn't happy about that but at least it gave me a great feeling of payback.

I didn't want to keep any of my things from the cottage. I wanted no physical reminders of my time with him. My mental scars were enough. Everything felt tainted and evil.

My sister was a huge help to me at this time. Leanne was good when it came to handling the police, and she told me she would accompany me to court if ever that was needed. She went to a car-boot sale with her friend to sell my stuff from the cottage. I sold some of it online. We hardly got any money for it but anything was a bonus. My mum handled the transfer of power over my other finances, so within a few weeks my benefits were returned to me.

The months that followed were extremely hard. I suffered flashbacks and deep anxiety. I went back on the medication I was taking before he'd ordered me to stop.

The police promised I'd have access to victim support, but when I enquired I found that only group-counselling sessions were offered. For someone with Asperger's, having been through what I had, it was completely unsuitable. I appreciate that resources are limited but I felt like they were only paying lip service to the notion of victim support. It was a one-size-fits-all service, with no room to accommodate people with particular issues or sensitivities.

They also said they would keep me constantly updated on the progress of the investigation, but they didn't, which caused me further anxiety. Every time I asked for an update they always made it seem like a chore.

Detective Inspector Robert Thornton was involved in my case from the beginning. After what seemed like an age, he informed me that the Crown Prosecution Service (CPS) were formally bringing charges against ST. He would face trial for false imprisonment and ten counts of rape.

I was devastated. What about the coercive behaviour, attacking me with a knife, the many more rapes and sexual assaults? DI Thornton said it was difficult for them and the CPS in cases where there is so much abuse in such a short space of time. He said that they had to cram it all into just a few charges because otherwise there would be too much to prosecute him with.

I didn't understand that logic. If they arrested a bank robber and found evidence of twenty banks he'd raided, would they only charge him with three?

It took nearly 18 months for the case to come to court. A date was finally set for November 2013 at Merthyr Tydfil Crown Court, before Judge Richard Twomlow. ST was pleading not guilty so it was going to trial. I should have known he would never admit to anything. Forcing me to give evidence was all part of his continuing control. The thought of having to see him again, perhaps across a courtroom, where I'd be made to recount the most horrible things that happened to me, gave me nightmares.

Finally having a date sparked a tumult of emotions. It was a relief to know that the case was finally moving forward and we were one step closer to him being off the streets for a long time. As the date drew nearer, however, my stress levels rose. The thought of facing him absolutely terrified me. I had panic attacks about giving evidence. What if I wasn't believed? What if he was found not guilty and was free to seek his revenge on me?

On the day of the trial I was a nervous wreck. I wasn't sure if I could go through with it. I arrived at the court with my family. I didn't know what to expect, as I'd had no guidance from the prosecution. We asked the court officials where we should go. They were very unfriendly and unsupportive. They showed us to a room where we could wait to be called. We walked in and I couldn't believe it. His mum and James were there. We immediately requested to be moved. The stress was unbelievable.

I had thought someone from the prosecution might help guide me through the process, but the first time I met with the Crown prosecutor was on the day of the court case. She was nice enough but didn't fill me with a lot of confidence. She said there were 'lots of people in the public gallery', which made me feel a hundred times more anxious. Why did she have to say that? There was a long delay before the trial started, and we were just left waiting. Nobody kept us informed of what was going on. I was starting to panic. The trial hadn't even started but already I was forming the opinion that the whole court process was not in favour of the victim. It was felt like it was designed to make it as hard as possible for the victim.

There was one bit of good news, however. I didn't have to give evidence in the courtroom itself. I would be sitting in a side room watching the proceedings via a video link. The video-recorded statement I gave to the police would be played as evidence, so I wasn't required to answer questions. That helped calm me down a little. At least I wouldn't have to face him.

The Crown prosecutor had introduced me to a witness-support officer and explained that she would sit in the evidence room with me. I thought she might be a reassuring voice during such a difficult time, but she barely spoke to me. All she did was examine the contents of her nose, take her shoes off and pick at her skin.

When the time came for the trial to start there was a further delay because they were experiencing problems with the video link. The court could see into our room, but I couldn't see or hear what was happening in court. Nobody really knew how to work the video, so when the images did finally appear the judge was upside down. It was a bit of a shambles.

The trial process was interminably slow, and the proceedings went into a second day and then a third. I attended court each day but it was frustrating, as I was largely kept in the dark about what was going on.

On the third day of the trial, however, the Crown prosecutor delivered a shock. ST's mum had decided to present to the court the letters she claimed I'd written to her son while he was in prison. ST's lawyer excitedly announced that it was vital new evidence, and the judge agreed to halt the trial so both sides had a chance to go over the letters and assess their significance. The prosecutor was concerned that the defence, armed with these letters, would be able to convince the jury that I was in love and a willing partner in the relationship. I couldn't believe it. Surely any juror would understand why I had to write those letters if given the proper context? Here was a violent, controlling abuser. He was in prison but only for a few weeks, and in no time he would be out and back to torment me. I had to write what he told me to otherwise he would have killed me. It was all part of coercive control. It made me so angry and frustrated. It was like they were living in the Stone Age. He'd controlled every aspect of my life. Every hour was accounted for.

I wanted the chance to explain that to the jury – and even my victim-support officer and one of the female inspectors didn't think it was a big deal – but the prosecutor wasn't having any of it. I was absolutely gutted. I cursed myself for not throwing the letters in the bin or burning them when I had the chance. I don't know why I didn't. My head was all over the place during that time.

I was suspicious about the supposed content of the letters. The ones I wrote had been typed on a computer but that wasn't how the police described them to me. Had someone doctored them in some way to make them even worse than they were? And what about the letters he'd sent me, which spelled out his demands? Were they submitted too? I doubted the court was getting the full picture.

My view counted for nothing. The prosecutor took the decision, in light of the letters, to drop the rape charges. She decided instead to offer his defence barrister a deal. If he pleaded guilty to the charge of false imprisonment, they would drop the other charges. The defence agreed. For them it was a huge result.

I was devastated. Nearly 18 months of preparation and tension, building to the trial and then this.

The charge he would be pleading guilty to was three days of false imprisonment. However, the reality was that I suffered many more days than that. That solitary charge didn't come close to telling the full story.

The prosecutor tried to make me see the positives. He was going to be convicted. The judge had the power to keep him in prison for a long time. This was a good thing. He would be off the streets and unable to hurt me or any other woman.

When Judge Richard Twomlow finally addressed the man who had raped, abused and controlled my life for two years, he said, 'You are a danger to all women.'

He sentenced ST – his real name is Simon Matthew Tibble – to be detained indefinitely under the Mental Health Act.

I was mentally scarred and bruised by the court process, but I would have to find a way to put it behind me. After the trial was over the police came to our house with two experts in mental-health detainees to explain what the sentence meant. Tibble, they said, was detained under the same Mental Health Act provision as Moors murderer Ian Brady. The Moors murders was one of the most high-profile cases in British criminal history. In 1966, Ian Brady and his accomplice Myra Hindley were convicted of the abduction, sexual assault and murder of Lesley Ann Downey, 10, John Kilbride, 12, and Edward Evans, 17. The victims' bodies were buried on Saddleworth Moor, near Manchester. Years later the killers confessed to the murders of two other children, Pauline Reade, 16, and Keith Bennett, 12.

The police said the judge saw Tibble as being that dangerous, and they – and the experts – explained to my parents and me that Tibble would be off the streets for at least 20 years. That made us feel a bit better. It might not have been the result I wanted but it was over. I was finally free of evil.

He had tried to destroy me, but he had failed. I was stronger than he or anyone else imagined.

It was time to start my life all over again.

Epilogue

Rebuilding my life has not been easy. And it was made a million times harder on 8 March 2017 when my mother received a letter from my Ministry of Justice Victim Liaison Officer.

'Dear Mrs Crockett,' it read, 'I am contacting you as (offender Simon) Tibble has applied for a Mental Health Tribunal to start having unescorted leave.'

The bottom fell out of my world. What happened to the 20 years we were promised?

When he was detained for an indefinite period I felt uneasy because, unlike a normal custodial tariff, there was no way of knowing how long it was for. I had to take the police and their experts at their word when they explained that it was a serious sentence. I sincerely hoped it meant more than the three years and four months he had now served.

Yet here we were. He was applying to be allowed out – to mingle with society.

The letter went on to ask my mother if she wanted to contribute to the tribunal and 'to request any protective measures in respect of Sophie'.

We certainly did want to contribute to the tribunal but had grave doubts about the impact it would have. My experience so far with the criminal justice system had not given me much confidence.

Nevertheless, I offered a statement to the tribunal saying how, three years on from his conviction, I still felt in fear for my life, that he still presented a danger to me. We went to see our local MP, Ann Clwyd, who also submitted a letter to them.

It had no impact.

On 4 July 2017, just a day short of five years since I escaped his torture in the cottage, we received another letter from the Ministry of Justice. It said 'the offender could soon be starting his overnight leave'. Although this would not be in the Rhondda Cynon Taff or Merthyr Tydfil areas and exclusion zones were in place – that is, an understanding that he couldn't come within a certain number of miles of my house – it was a massive shock to think he was now free to roam the streets.

When we asked why he had been considered for occasional release we were told he had been showing signs of improvement. I thought back to the time he was in St Tydfil Hospital, when I saw him put on his act and give the doctors what they wanted. I knew he had done exactly the same this time.

Learning that he was out of detention was the biggest shock I have ever had in my life, like a punch in the face. I could barely catch my breath.

I am hugely sceptical about how much rehabilitation could be achieved in less than three-and-a-half years. I hope I am proved wrong, but I believe he still presents a danger to women. Every day I live in fear that at some point he will exact his revenge on me for locking him up. In my opinion it is not a case of if he does it again, it is a case of *when*.

He was a ticking time-bomb and nothing the Ministry of Justice can tell me about his supposed rehabilitation will convince me he has changed.

After a while, he was fully released from prison and supposedly moved into a halfway house in Bridgend, south Wales, where I believe his mum lived. What he will do or where he will go is something I won't find out, as victims of crime are only given the most limited of information.

Much of what I understand about Simon Tibble I have had to find out for myself. It was only many months after meeting him that I discovered he was a father to two children. There were issues there with his ex-partner because, I understand, he was not allowed access to his children. He had a relationship with his mum, but he does not get on with her partner and was not on speaking terms with his own father. He had one brother who lived in England, who he does not have a relationship with. His own family have issues with him but the Ministry of Justice is happy to release him into the wider community.

In the period since his conviction I have tried to get on with my life but it is a continual struggle. I have contemplated suicide many times, as I felt that, ultimately, it could provide my only escape from him. There have been times when I have not seen any other way out, and many times when I've thought I've lost my own sanity.

I suffer from severe post-traumatic stress disorder and suffer flashbacks all the time. I cannot eat, sleep or concentrate, and I struggle to connect with the people around me. I am deeply suspicious of people's intent and feel I cannot take anyone at face value anymore, after what he did to me. I feel like an outcast, as I have experienced things that other people wouldn't imagine, even in their worst nightmares.

It took me a long time to realise what this man did to me. He identified a vulnerable victim, saw me as prey, worked his way into my life, isolated me from the people who could protect me, groomed me and then subjected me to the most vile forms of physical, sexual and emotional abuse imaginable. None of the sex with him had been consented to, instigated or welcomed by me. He raped me, repeatedly, from the outset.

This is why I feel so strongly about telling my story. I could have remained anonymous. That is one right afforded to the victims of sexual crime. I have waived that right in the hope that my story might carry greater impact. I want to show people what he did to me, what signs to look out for if a man behaves in a certain way.

Another reason I wanted my story to be told was to highlight the inadequacies of the criminal justice system when dealing with victims of sexual abuse. I can't help but think back to that first interview with the police and the fact that it was cut short. It meant there were episodes that never got mentioned, things he could have been charged with.

I have issues with how the police and prosecution handle sensitive witnesses. Great steps have been taken in recent years but so much more needs to be done. In my experience, I was told one thing and then they did the complete opposite. I was told I would never have to worry about him ever again, but here we are. The way they treated me made me feel like I was worthless. It has felt at times like, rather than being there to serve the needs of the victims of crime, they were vultures pecking away at me.

Much is made of the support offered to victims of crime, but in practice it is poor. I didn't feel like I had proper, meaningful support, and I felt that there was a lack of sensitivity to people with mental-health issues. In my experience the victim is the one being punished at the moment; the criminal has everything given to them. In prison he will have had access to all sorts of programmes and so-called rehabilitation schemes. All he would have to do is go to the sessions, comply with the guidelines and tick the right boxes. I saw first-hand how he can act the part when called upon. He admitted to me that he knows how to play the game. Why can't the authorities see that? Would it not be better to learn from the victims what their attackers are like?

The judge said he was a 'danger to all women'. I'm sure when he said that he didn't mean he would be fine, though, as long as he had a bit of counselling. His behaviour was deep-rooted. He saw me as a sex object, something to manipulate and control. This was psychotic behaviour, not a relationship gone sour. It was meticulously planned and executed. The thought of how he has manipulated and abused the system in much the same way makes me angry and, at times, hysterical.

We were offered lots of support. But it turned out to be just words. I asked if my family could be moved to another council house so he wouldn't know where to find me. Nothing happened. I asked if it was possible to change my name. Nothing happened. I asked about the sort of protection we could get. We were given an alarm for our house that was supposed to send a signal to a police station if it went off. It did go off a few times, which gave us all a fright, but on each occasion the police never showed up. If that had been a real attacker I could have been killed and the police would never have caught the perpetrator.

To the criminal justice system we are the voiceless. The victims of crime are abandoned beforehand and abandoned afterwards. We are just left on the sidelines. That is, unless we speak up. In my mind, the whole system needs to change so that the criminal actually gets punished for the crimes they have committed and the lives they have ruined.

Simon Tibble has served a pitiful sentence and is out of prison. In stark contrast, I am the one serving a life sentence. He made me a prisoner. I have to live with the abuse and torment he put me through for the rest of my life. I am the one being punished. There have been moments when I've felt like I can't go on. Yet, somehow, I have been able to carve out something of a life for myself.

During the period he was detained I was scared to leave the house, and doing anything new made me as anxious as I'd felt when I was a little girl. Being trapped in that house of horrors had left me emotionally scarred. I lived in fear that the explicit images he took of me would surface somewhere online.

In my early life I loved reading, had a thirst for knowledge and took an obsessive interest in a wide variety of subjects. I loved writing poetry and had turned my hand to writing short stories. He crushed all that. He didn't want a woman who read – to him that was dangerous. I might form ideas, read accounts from other women who have been the victims of abuse and try to find a way to leave him. He wanted me dumb and mute. The oppressive conditions inside that house made it easy for him. Living in near darkness or ultra-violet light messes with your mind. Your eyes dry out and your head throbs. The last thing I could do was read. At one stage I feared I might go blind.

Although I have been out of that situation for nearly seven years now, I am still experiencing the after-effects. My eyesight isn't great. I get headaches and struggle to focus when reading.

And yet, despite everything, I slowly began to rediscover my old self. I started reading books for a very short period at a time, which rekindled my love of learning. I've always been interested in science – a passion that was nearly destroyed forever by him – and gradually that fascination was reawakened within me.

As a young child I was extremely sensitive to the psychic world. An expert once labelled me an indigo child. Yet when I was under his control and suffering extreme levels of abuse I felt I had closed down spiritually. It was only at the very end – when I prayed to God and the angels and they provided me with the means to escape through that little Furby – that I felt I still had my spiritual voice.

Now I am able to have more spiritual experiences because I am away from him. I give readings to my family, and in the future I would like to give spiritual readings to the general public.

In addition to this, I am now a trained child counsellor, a cognitive behavioural therapist and mindfulness therapist and I hope to be able to use my experiences to help other vulnerable people.

As someone without a formal education, it seemed a forlorn hope that I might one day achieve something with my life. However, I began doing some remote learning with the Open University. As I completed modules and got back into the habit of studying, I eventually managed to attain a diploma in science. Not bad for someone who left school aged ten.

I didn't want to stop there. I scored so well on my UCAS exam that I decided to apply to universities. I landed an interview with Cardiff University, but in early 2019 I accepted an unconditional offer from another university to study cellular and molecular medicine.

Studying has saved my life. Without it I don't know what I would have done. I was in danger of sinking into a depression so deep that I might not have recovered.

The thought of going to university is a daunting one. I don't do friends and my natural instinct is to keep my distance from people. I prefer to be alone with my parents. I can communicate with people but usually that's as far as it goes. I have never known what it is like to have a proper friend.

I often find it easier to communicate online. The remoteness helps my confidence. I like the barrier in between. And I did manage to strike up a conversation with a man online. Naturally, I was wary of sharing any private information with him, but over time he proved himself to be caring, sympathetic and understanding. It took a lot of courage for me to meet him, but the more time we spent together the more I began to trust again. I am pleased to say that I am now in a very loving relationship with a man who would do anything for me and is very understanding. He loves me and cares about me completely.

In the beginning of the relationship there were a lot of hurdles we had to overcome. Having PTSD means even the smallest trigger can spark an anxiety attack. I have no way of knowing how and when these attacks will present themselves. Even something as seemingly insignificant as a lampshade can induce a panic attack, if it is the same as one we had in the cottage. It is like negotiating a minefield, but slowly we are learning to cope.

When I look back on my life, I often wonder how and why a succession of people felt they could treat me so badly: the TV psychic, the tutor, the mobile-phone man, my dance instructor and, of course, Simon Tibble. All of these people have manipulated me in some way at the very least, and at worst they have acted criminally.

It has made me realise that there are people out there who can immediately sense when someone is vulnerable, and they prey on that. People need to be aware; parents, especially, need to be aware of this.

Even though I had problems before I was nine years old, everything seemed so much simpler then. Yes, there were times I felt like an alien and even that I had been adopted, but I was an innocent child in a bubble that I thought would never pop.

That existence was shattered the second I met Tibble. He was out and out controlling from the very beginning, but he hid behind an ability to be charming. Everything he did at the outset – holding my hand, cosying up to me, moving me away from other people, both physically and figuratively, was all part of a wider plan.

From that very first encounter on his doorstep I believe he identified me as vulnerable – someone he could prey on. It was like he could detect that I was unable to speak up and unlikely to tell anyone about anything.

He completely took over my life and controlled my every movement. He turned me away from my family. He totally messed with my head. He made me think he was practically God and his word was all that mattered.

Compliments, adoration, being needed … He made out that I was the love of his life and the centre of his universe, which I felt was a lot of pressure, but he managed to worm his way in and become a permanent fixture straight away.

My fate was sealed from the moment he held my hand. A more streetwise person would have instantly pulled away, but I didn't because I didn't know if I should. While I was having an internal debate about whether this was normal or he was just being nice or I should be wary, he was plotting several moves ahead.

I still feel like I will see him again some day. I live in fear of a revenge attack. I suppose I always will.

I am not unique in being a victim of sexual and psychological abuse. According to Rape Crisis England and Wales, approximately 85,000 women and 12,000 men (aged 16 to 59) experience rape, attempted rape or sexual assault by penetration in England and Wales alone every year; that's roughly 11 of the most serious sexual offences (experienced by adults alone) every hour. Only around 15 per cent of those who experience sexual violence report it to the police.

Conviction rates for rape are far lower than they are for other crimes, with only 5.7 per cent of reported rape cases ending in a conviction. Changes to the bail system in 2017 have made it even harder for women to come forward. The changes have introduced lots of bureaucratic hoops the police have to jump through when they put people on bail. Most suspects are released without any bail conditions, so there is nothing to stop them contacting the complainant or going to her home address while the police investigation is ongoing.

Statistics show that 90 per cent of rape victims know the perpetrator prior to the offence, and in the majority of cases there has often already been a long history of repeat behaviour. Therefore it's vital to keep the parties apart so the women aren't intimidated. Women who are victims of sex crimes already feel vulnerable and scared. The system should be designed to protect them – not put them at more risk.

A lack of resources is also a massive problem for police units dealing with sexual offences and domestic abuse. Resources have been going down at a time when the number of women reporting offences to the police has been going up. If the trend continues women will be discouraged from coming forward, and criminals like Tibble will get off scot-free.

I know only too well how hard it is to speak out, but only by doing so will our voices be heard.

I want to take this opportunity to address any victims of sexual abuse out there who might read my story and see similarities to their own situation. This is my letter to you.

Dear You,

When I was in this difficult situation I felt confused and that there was no way out for me. I felt like I had been sucked into a black hole and there was no escape. I felt like I was in a place far out of reach of everyone, being totally controlled like a marionette.

When I found the courage to leave it took a long time for these feelings to go. It isn't going to happen overnight and not many people will understand. It's a hard road but I can't emphasise enough how much it's worth it. I managed to combat these feelings by studying; I got my qualifications via distance learning and got into medical school. I studied long into the night. It gave me a focus. It gave me something to achieve. You may find something else that helps you, but keep focusing on the positive and remember to take baby steps – don't run before you can walk. It's going to take time, but remember it is not a race.

My advice to you would be to try everything you can to leave the abusive situation and the abusive person. Seek help – there is help out there, people will help you. You are strong, much stronger than you think. You will come through this. You deserve to be loved and respected. It

will be hard at first but it will get better. Even
though I may not be there with you physically to
help you, please know you're in my thoughts
day and night.

It is going to be okay. Just take that very first
step to freedom and you're on your way.

Yours,

Sophie

Next, and finally, I would like to address the person who
tried to destroy me.

Dear ST,

When I ran away from you on that day back in
2012 I told myself that I would never see you
again, that I would do everything in my power to
keep you away from me – and I have.

When you met me I was a little girl who knew
nothing of the world. I was innocent, naïve and
thought people like you didn't exist. How wrong
I was.

You broke me down, left me powerless, had
me doubting my sanity. You made me want to
murder you and kill myself as well.

You had all this power and control over me,
but let me tell you something now: I am not that
little girl anymore.

Admittedly, you took away a part of me that I will probably never get back, and left an empty place inside of me where I always see the worst in people and situations, always the darkness and never the light.

I am a grown woman now, and I have proven my strength and bravery.

I have done things that I never thought I would be able to do, and because of all the things you put me through, nothing scares me now. I can do anything.

I want you to know what I think of you, as it's long overdue. I think you are a sexual predator, an idiot and a loser.

When I was a child I thought you were intelligent, but now that I am a woman I know that you aren't. You hold no special powers; you are just a child groomer.

You are a strange person who will live a lonely life and never be happy. Yes, I have wished for your death, but that gives you time in my mind and I don't even want to give you that satisfaction. I want to forget you completely because you are not worth any of my time, not even my thoughts.

I hope you will never treat anyone else the way you treated me. Stay away from children, stay away from women, and remember what the Crown Court judge said about you: 'You are a danger to all women.'

I am now in a loving relationship and, even though I will never be able to completely forget the things you did to me as a child, I know that I am successful and you will never be.

Goodbye, pathetic man, and remember, no one mourns the wicked.

Your survivor,

Sophie

Moving Memoirs

Stories of hope, courage and the power of love…

If you loved this book, then you will love our Moving Memoirs eNewsletter

Sign up to…

- Be the first to hear about new books

- Get sneak previews from your favourite authors

- Read exclusive interviews

- Be entered into our monthly prize draw to win one of our latest releases before it's even hit the shops!

Sign up at

www.moving-memoirs.com